Beating Uncertainty

7 winning strategies to manage insecurity in life & business

Mohamed Elshahawy

BEATING UNCERTAINTY
www.beatinguncertainty.com

Copyright © 2017 Mohamed Elshahawy
ISBN: 978-1-77277-137-4

All rights reserved. No portion of this book may be reproduced mechanically, electronically, or by any other means, including photocopying, without permission of the publisher or author except in the case of brief quotations embodied in critical articles and reviews. It is illegal to copy this book, post it to a website, or distribute it by any other means without permission from the publisher or author.

Limits of Liability and Disclaimer of Warranty
The author and publisher shall not be liable for your misuse of the enclosed material. This book is strictly for informational and educational purposes only.

Warning – Disclaimer
The purpose of this book is to educate and entertain. The author and/or publisher do not guarantee that anyone following these techniques, suggestions, tips, ideas, or strategies will become successful. The author and/or publisher shall have neither liability nor responsibility to anyone with respect to any loss or damage caused, or alleged to be caused, directly or indirectly by the information contained in this book.

Publisher
10-10-10 Publishing
Markham, ON
CANADA

Printed in Canada and The United States of America

Table of Contents

DEDICATION	v
ACKNOWLEDGEMENTS	vii
FOREWORD	ix
PREFACE	xi
CHAPTER 1: THE UNCERTAINTY SYNDROME	1
CHAPTER 2: FACE THE REALITY	11
CHAPTER 3: ALIGN WITH "CHANGE"	25
CHAPTER 4: LEAD THE TRANSFORMATION	35
CHAPTER 5: STAY SHARPLY FOCUSED	45
CHAPTER 6: RETHINK YOUR STRATEGY	57
CHAPTER 7: TAKE RISK	69
CHAPTER 8: BE RESILIENT	81
CHAPTER 9: BE SIMPLE	93
CHAPTER 10: BE PART OF THE EXPERIENCE	105
ABOUT THE AUTHOR	115

For Radwa

ACKNOWLEDGEMENTS

I would first like to acknowledge my late father, *Ahmed El-Shahawy*, whose guidance was always quiet and assured..

I'm indebted to my beautiful mother, *Amina Hassan*, for being a role model for me. I would not have been able to achieve all my success without her unconditional love and endless support. Her amazing positivity and resilience always have been a great source of inspiration to me and many others.

Thanks to my wife *Radwa*, to whom I dedicate this book, and my amazing and wonderful three boys, *Ali, Abdulrhman and Hussein*, who fill my life with love and happiness.

I'm grateful to every man and woman who is facing uncertainty with faith and insight and who gave me the inspiration and wisdom that I have expressed in this book. As in this book, I present many stories shared with me by friends, neighbors, and other people I have met or heard about around the world, especially during the last six years of my life. In few cases, I've changed the names to protect the privacy of individuals.

I extend my acknowledgment to all those with whom I am working, or have worked, especially at the innovative leading company 3M, where I learned a lot and where I was always motivated to give my best to stay in leadership.

And last but not least, I'm so grateful for the wonderful team of professionals who helped me achieve this book for you. Special thanks for *Rosa Greco*, my special book architect, for her great support.

FOREWORD

Your inability to live with life's "unknowns" can lead you to worry and cause you stress. Accordingly, in order to control these feelings, you need to first accept being uncertain, and then you need to take the right actions to decrease the uncertainty. It's always obvious when you, personally, cannot fully understand the present or are unable to predict the future. Thus, it impacts your daily decisions about business, relationships and the quality of your life.

Mohamed Elshahawy has been embracing many dramatic changes in his life, and his exciting life dynamic has allowed him to deeply understand the concept of change management and has shown him how to master uncertainty in his life and business. *Beating Uncertainty* will demonstrate to you how you can align with change and lead the inevitable situations occurring in your life.

Mohamed believes that when dealing with uncertainty there is nothing more important than focusing on yourself. He has painted a map for you to discover self-awareness and has created a positive mind setting approach for you to be able to pursue happiness in your life.

Within *Beating Uncertainty*, Mohamed will discuss with you three essential things:

Firstly, Mohamed will reveal your common restraints which might drastically impact your decision making, performance, and the achievements in your life.

Secondly, Mohamed will teach you several important enablers, which will be effective weapons in your fight against uncertainty in your life and business.

Thirdly, you will be intrigued by a set of strategic moves, which will allow you to enhance both your efficiency and effectiveness in your life and support your work in hitting your targets, in spite of any potential risks.

Beating Uncertainty is a brilliant navigational tool, specially designed to help you master uncertainty and beat all its hostility.

Raymond Aaron
New York Times Bestselling Author

PREFACE

It was 2007 when I became curious about how business is reacting to the global financial calamity. In 2008, the plight of the global financial crisis was massive. Many financial and business institutions were trying to manage the situation through different strategies and leadership approaches. In 2009, it became easier to see how some organizations succeeded in absorbing the shock of this crisis, while others failed. Being part of the experiment, at my position, I learned a lot from that unfortunate situation, especially on the business management side.

In the following years -- without necessarily being linked to the global financial crisis -- many political and social changes took place in the world, in the way that made it look more uncertain than ever before! In 2011, public democratic uprisings arose independently and spread across the Arab world. The movement, which is known as the Arab Spring, originated in Tunisia in December 2010, and quickly took place in Egypt, Libya, Syria, Yemen, Bahrain, Saudi Arabia, and Jordan.

While this movement has almost failed to reach its goals in most of the countries where it has originally sparked, the whole world is living the drawback of its letdown, as on the humanitarian side, we are living the biggest refugee and displacement crisis of this time. Meantime we observe the massive economic regression in many of what was supposed to be part of the emerging economies that was supposed to compensate economic slowdown in other parts of the world.

At another part of the world, and in synchronization with the Arab spring, the first occupy protest "which is an international socio-political movement against social inequality and lack of 'real democracy' around the world" received widespread attention when it took place in New York City in September 2011, under the name of Occupy Wall Street. By October, occupy protests had taken place in over 951 cities across 82 countries, and over 600 communities in the United States.

On June 23, 2016, British citizens voted to exit the European Union. The referendum roiled global markets, including currencies, causing the British pound to fall to its lowest level in decades. The future of the United Kingdom as well as the European Union became a question mark as a result.

Before the end of the same year, many people around the world were shocked by the election of Donald J. Trump as president of the United States. The incident that created a global wave of uncertainty, due to his lack of political experience, bigotry values, and his positions against Muslims, Mexicans, disabled persons, and women. Many believe that he might take the world to a new war.

The previous events took place while other major global conditions were, and still threaten you, me, and the whole world; for example, climate change and the global rise in human infectious disease outbreaks that is resulting in many international public health emergencies.

At a personal level, during the last few years, like many others, I was living in an aggravated sense of uncertainty about almost everything in life. I had to leave my home, my extended family, my job, and my country because of the socio-political turmoil and lack of personal security that was occurring back home. Moving from one country to another, establishing new relationships, learning new languages, settling my family in many different places and exhausting trials to restore my lifestyle again was like sailing through the mighty ocean.

I have become more convinced that it is not the "uncertainty" itself that could make your life stressful; but it is the anxiety and the fear stemming from that uncertainty. Especially when investing in the relationship between uncertainty and fear becomes a good business for some politicians and decision makers around the world.

Uncertainty creates endotoxins, which can take you down completely, with no power to fight your life battle. Victims of uncertainty are more likely to have what I call *the uncertainty syndrome*, which is manifested as an enduring feeling of anxiety mixed with muddy thinking, complex communication, fear of conflict, and fixation on the past.

Your battle against uncertainty will not end by completely eradicating it from your life, as this is impossible, but you beat uncertainty when you prevent it from limiting your choices in life and restricting you from pursuing happiness.

My purpose for writing this book is to share with you some winning life strategies that can enable you to win your battle against the lethal power of uncertainty in life and business. Although I take into consideration the rich theoretical knowledge about the concept of "uncertainty" and the modern application of it as an organizational discipline in the micro economy, I focus more on bringing you a set of individual strategic enablers that will make you victorious in your battle against uncertainty.

CHAPTER 1

THE UNCERTAINTY SYNDROME

Uncertainty is a situation in which the current state of knowledge is such that the order or nature of things is unknown; the consequences, extent, or magnitude of circumstances, conditions or events is unpredictable and credible probabilities to possible outcomes cannot be assigned. In another meaning it is the absence of confidence or conciseness in one's ideas, judgments, or aims. Feeling Uncertain of something contains a significant amount of worry, and a core feature of worry is the inability to tolerate uncertainty! In fact, when you are anxious you say to yourself that you would rather know for sure that the outcome will be bad than be left in suspense. That means when intolerance of uncertainty is a problem, anxiety is the result. This state usually develops a set of concurrent emotions or actions that usually form an identifiable pattern of personal and organizational limitations. In this chapter, I will discuss with you some common restraints that usually emerge with uncertainty and work to complicate your life as they impact your decision-making process, worsen your performance and delay your achievement. These restraints are:

Fear of conflict

"Nothing is clear or safe nowadays so you shouldn't slip into conflicts or confrontations about such issues!" This is what your subconscious mind tells you during uncertain times. This reminds me of the famous wisdom that says "We only fear what we haven't understood." Studies on the biology of fear and anxiety tell you that fear or anxiety results in the expression of a range of adaptive or defensive behaviors, which are aimed at escaping from the source of danger or motivational conflict.

Do you have some resistance to conflict? So for example; Instead of addressing issues directly, do you try to be "nice" and end up spending an excessive amount of time talking to yourself or others; complaining, feeling frustrated, ruminating on something that already happened, or anticipating something that may happen? In fact, monitoring your conflict avoidance is the first step to moving past it. Below are examples of daily conflict avoidance statements that could be found in your workplace or any other places.

"Someone has to tell my business partner that his impulsive decisions are worsening the profitability of the operation, but I'm dreading it. I've been thinking about it all day and haven't been able to get anything done."

"I know what they're going to say — that we can't have more resources due to budget constraints. I'll probably just give up on this."

Conflict avoidance can often show up as ignoring the issue, or overlooking "the elephant inside the room." In business situation this elephant could be the absence of certain essential resources, knowledge, or legislation.

Generally in life, conflict avoidance can take place by side-stepping the clash and changing the subject when the conflict comes up, such as what sometimes happen between husband and wife when discussing a critical issue. Another manifestation is the complete withdrawal to avoid conflict, as when seeing a mistake or corrupt action from a higher level. Just like a turtle retreating into its shell.

When you are dealing with conflicts, it is advisable to take the focus off you and your fear, and concentrate on what the business needs. Nothing personal; it is all about the issue at hand. Tackle it courageously and speak up. Use observations, not labels, while keeping a calm manner. Always remember, the more you expose yourself to conflict the better you become at handling it. Conflicts management generally makes you strong in negotiation and communication; you will feel more practical and flexible if you go positively through conflicting matters. And here is the good news for you: conflicts leads to solutions and consequently that should reduce your uncertainty and helps you moving forward in life and business.

Muddy thinking

The overwhelming fear of many things in today's life, like the fear of economic collapse, unemployment, government surveillance, sickness and old age or fear of a terrorist attack can make your life a real uncertain life, especially since not much has changed in this regard during the last few years. With anxiety about all the above, you may get confused about priorities, goals, what is right and what is wrong. And all of that can muddy your thinking. Muddy thinking can jeopardize your success, and your plans may get stuck in some of this mud.

So, in a business or a life situation, the simplest explanation that covers all the facts will usually offer the best solution, but uncovering it might not be quite so easy. That is why you need to be sure of your personal values which define your role in life, and tell others what you consider important. For example ethics, integrity, professionalism, teamwork, and relationships express what you value, and dictate most of your actions in life.

You should in addition have clear answers to questions like; what are your strengths versus your limitations? What is your passion? What is your ultimate dream and who is your role model? What are your plans for your personal life, career, and family? From where should you start? Where do you need to go, and what is your backup plan?

When you approach a problem stop trying to make all aspects of the situation you face top priority and loop around the periphery of that problem instead of cutting to the core of it. When you take decisions learn how to separate what is serious from what is insignificant. On the whole, creating clear, sharp vision about the situation you are facing is your responsibility, and becomes more important when you are leading others.

It is not enough to have the enthusiasm and the desire for the action; you need to plan, otherwise you are taking a big risk, for yourself and for your organization. Your structured mind, in addition to a well-crafted life vision based on strong core values, will make you more successful in beating uncertain life.

Hooking on details

Imagine that you have taken a snapshot for your life during an uncertain time; how would it appear? I think it will be as if it had been taken by the camera's "aperture priority" mode with a subject in focus but the background blurry. Uncertainty makes the overall picture of your life hazy and pushes you to focus on the details which unfortunately evolve more during major changes.

If so, then you need to give it more attention in order to guarantee that those tiny little details are not distracting you from achieving your bigger goals. Actually, details might not be your enemy, but they could be your foolish friend who wastes your time, drains your energy and hinders your progress. Some days, it can feel like you're drowning in trivialities, totally detached from the "bigger work" that you feel called to do! You start looping inside a frustrating vicious circle that makes you uncertain about your future. To overcome such situation and break this vicious circle you need a simple yet effective strategy to keep you focusing on important things rather than focusing on distracting things. Here is how to make it work:

Live your dream and do whatever it takes to reach it by Linking all that you want to your bigger dream and making sure it is always present, visualized and memorized. Have the right estimation for the work needed, including all the preparation and details. Create the habit of recording your daily achievements and the actions you took towards your dream.

Prioritize and execute immediately. First, make a list of everything that's distracting you, things to remember, things to research later, ideas you don't want to forget and save your list for later. Second, ask yourself the following questions: What is most important to do first? What has to be done so others can work? What will cause the most trouble if I haven't finished? Then, sit down and focus on the big task at hand—knowing that all of the "other stuff" are safe and secure, preserved on your list for later. Finally, manage important details immediately yet delegate less important ones.

Practice the selective focus by going deep in the field you are working on and concentrating on the specific task you want to accomplish while keeping other parts clearly out of your focus. The amount of results that you will achieve in a short time will surprise you, but remember to take some time to have mind rest before coming back to intense focus.

Tiding to the past

When the future is not clear as what happened during major changes in life or business you often find yourself more attached to the past. This could be manifested when you repeatedly recall your past achievements or go in deep nostalgia to the old days. It is good to understand that both positive and negative past experiences have helped to shape who you are today but you cannot change things that are in the past, you can only change the part they play in your future. With this in mind and in order to prevent your past from controlling your future, you need to put it firmly where it belongs -- behind you, a memory with no power to influence your future. Generally don't try to replicate experiences that worked well in different circumstances, or took place in the past, assuming they will work well in completely different situations and time.

Don't make the mistake of using your past as reason or excuse for your failure to achieve your goals. Living the past is a dull and lonely business. Looking back strains your neck muscles, causing you to bump into people not going your way. Your life is not the same as it was last year, nor will it be the same next year so make an intentional choice to control uncertainty, and take back your power focusing on here and now

Narrow mind thinking

A real negative aspect of uncertainty is its power to ratify narrow band thinking within some people, especially when they live the overwhelming anxiety that results from major life changes. Narrow thinking can consequently reduce your problem-solving power, and increase your feelings of uncertainty.

Have you ever thought about your thinking habits, or done an honest self-analysis to check whether you are a "narrow-minded" person or not?

Are you regularly willing to listen to or tolerate other people's views? Think about your own frames in life, business, religion, social relations, politics, or any other things; do you often think out of these frames? Are you open to new ideas not similar to what your family or social class usually adopt? If you have one or more of the following signs, it means you're somehow a narrow-minded person:

1. You take everything personally.

You can't accept criticism regarding your actions. Either in work or family you understand opposing opinion to mean that someone doesn't like you or is against you. Or in another word, you dislike anyone who disagrees with you.

2. You're obsessed with righteousness.

You like to be right, fit and ceremonious on all occasions, even though you know that you are not like this because you have defects and shortcomings like any human being. If you cannot apologize for something, laugh at your inaccuracy with near and dear ones, or openly accept your mistakes, it is certainly a sign of narrow-mindedness.

3. You are closed to new ideas.

A narrow-minded person may appear conservative, liberal, religious or spiritual on the surface. Deep down, however, such a person lives inside a closed shell, unwilling to expose himself to new opinions even if they're based on facts and obvious realities.

4. You're judgmental.

You become judgmental, or to a worse extent discriminatory or racist, to anyone different or special. Dissatisfaction and uncertainty probably accompany this, due to the practice of guessing more than analyzing.

5. You don't like to socialize or network with others.

Socializing at work or generally in life is not your comfort zone, even with social media such as Facebook, LinkedIn or Twitter.

Truly when you have a biased, bigoted, intolerant, or prejudiced viewpoint you are inviting conflicts as well as hindering many opportunities in life and business, and living with a significant amount of uncertainty. However, for some people, narrow-mindedness could be a way to maintain order and avoid chaos through protecting their "comfort zone!"

All the above was a trial to define uncertainty and outline the common glitches associated with it. But is uncertainty all bad or does it include some useful aspects? Isn't it better to deal with uncertainty as a fact of life? That is what I'm going to discuss with you in the next chapter of this book.

CHAPTER 2

FACE THE REALITY

Uncertainty is part of the game of life. Living in situations that involve imperfect and unknown information is what makes life as it is: imperfect, demanding and tempting. Your inability to fully understand an existing situation or predicting its future outcomes, or even see the past as a definitive fact, is a basic feature of you as a human in this life, and as an individual who struggles to be convinced of the validity, truthfulness, or evidence of a proposition or idea. Truly, your human tendency to want to be sure of the reliability of certain statement or condition will never stop.

Humans are bombarded with uncertainty throughout their everyday lives, and resolving this uncertainty is a primary motive in people's lives (Kagan, 1972). The resolution of uncertainty occurs through the identification of relationships between environmental cues and subsequent outcomes. (Alloy & Tabachnik, 1984)

Unlike "believing" which is possible without warrant or evidence, "certainty" implies having valid evidence or proof. Thus, when you fail to obtain this, uncertainty becomes associated with a sense of anxiety of a possible future outcome. It's very obvious when you face a life situation that you cannot fully understand, or are unable to predict its future impact. With this in mind, all you need is to do two things:

First: to accept being uncertain

It needs braveness to walk into a situation knowing you won't be able to judge your decisions until you've either succeeded or failed. Either in business or in life you'll many times crave to have the perfect amount of information needed to take a decision, but be careful as this might paralyze you from moving forward. So you have to learn how to use your subconscious mind to have a kind of solution, or at least a direction to follow. Yes, follow your gut feeling. There is no such thing as a purely logical decision. In fact your brain uses a combination of logic and emotion when making decisions of any kind. That specific emotion, innate to you as human, is the intuition. You must recognize this instinct within you and develop it the right way, as it might be your only navigation tool during uncertainty.

Second: to take actions to reduce uncertainty

Aim to achieve incremental growth by creating a series of short-term plans that can evolve as the situation becomes clearer. By this way, you can reduce uncertainty while avoiding the risks that come with making a big, broad decision. In addition use external opinion to avoid blind spots in your journey through ambiguity.

Generally be motivated for the unknown; experiment and even willingly include yourself in the new experiment. Reach out into the future for solutions, information, or hunches. Always explore, both in conversation and practical situations

The real challenge

Einstein said, "The most important decision we make is whether we believe we live in a friendly or hostile universe." So which do you believe, friendly or hostile? You might see the world around you as a friendly and peaceful world, where people around you exchange compassion and respect with each other, the hostility is low, and security exists in most of life aspects. Or maybe you see it the opposite way, as annoying, full of conspiracy, intimidation, and violence. Or maybe you don't really know and think it could be both, or neither. For me, I see the whole question from a different angle as it always depends on your way of thinking. If you are frequently looking for threats and enemies, you will find them and vice versa. In the same way, you can see uncertainty in life and business either as an enemy or as a friend. Uncertainty can be a demotivating fact of life that can overwhelm and frustrate you, or it can be a real motivation to explore the world around you, to learn and expand. In all cases, uncertainty usually carries with it a considerable load of anxiety and distress, and it is up to you to resist or to surrender. Having the right attitude to resolve uncertainty in life is your way to beating its hostile nature. In fact, you can't change or control what is happening in the world. You can only change or control your own reaction and behaviour towards it. Thus, living with faith, hope, and curiosity for the unknown is what makes uncertainty in life a real motivator.

The most beautiful sea hasn't been crossed yet.
The most beautiful child hasn't grown up yet.
The most beautiful days we haven't seen yet.
And the most beautiful words I wanted to tell you
I haven't said yet...
"Nazim Hikmat 1902-1963"

Let go of your old plan

In this uncertain world, what is the best way to achieve lifelong security and accomplish the objectives you really care about? The answer, in my opinion, is by letting go of your old plans and shifting your approach to the future.

Is going to university, having a degree, having some training programs, and finding a job in a decent organization, guarantee you a prosperous life in our today's life? Is your regular financial plan guaranteeing you safe retirement and secure future? I really doubt it! As In today's uncertain times, your traditional education, including most of what you have been taught in schools, universities and from your parents, is no longer a key for future success. Not because it is all wrong, but because it deals with a "predictable future" based on historical life analysis.

When I was a kid I used to see the future through the eyes of my parents and teachers, who got their knowledge from older generations. When I grew up I started to work my plans accordingly. I went through traditional - but relatively good- education, graduated with a university degree, did my MBA, and worked in some big companies. By the age of forty I had accumulated some savings, along with some investments. All that I accomplished in my life till that moment was based on a previous forecast for the future, based on a belief that what had worked for others in their past should also work for me in my future. But did it really work as i imagined? Absolutely not.

While most of my generation was stuck in the same traditional education, the whole world was changing, due to the booming revolution in information technology, and communication. There were fast and massive changes taking place in every life aspect. Complete markets became outdated. Many specialties were no longer needed. Commonly desired career competencies were replaced by new ones.

There were also some regional, massive, unpredictable or even hard to expect political and socio-economic changes that took place all around my family and me, which had forced me to move from one destination to another. On the other hand, the aggressive political turmoil in the area where I used to live and work had ruined my business and eroded my personal investments. I had to leave my home country, extended family and best friends to start from zero with a different culture, career, and people.

Success or happiness in life is a very personal and relative thing. The expensive lesson that I got to learn from all that I went through is just forget about your old life plans. Build a new and fresh understanding of your present and your future, since you are living in a highly changing and uncertain world that is not necessarily a bad one, but just different than the old one. So here is the strategy that made me -- again -- feel revitalized, happy and achieving:

Follow your "moving passion" whenever it serves your life purpose

If following your passion is making you happy and fulfilled, then awesome. If following your passion isn't working out or you have no idea what your passion is, then maybe it's time to revisit your core values and ask yourself what your life purpose is. When you find it most probably you'll find your passion there. Then pour your passion, resources, and plans on it and keep moving on from one completion to another.

Build the needed enablers for achievement through deep learning, coaching and mentorship

In fact, deep learning is the key for success in our today's life. Deep learners aim to understand the meaning of the text and interact with the material by creating relevant arguments and examples related to their daily lives. Meantime, most successful people, every time, everywhere, have coaches who support them in achieving a specific personal or professional goal by providing training, advice, and guidance. In today's life, you need to have a formal or informal relationship with someone who has the right experience and ability to teach you how to do things efficiently. Approaching new changes needs a mentor to provide you with psychosocial support, career guidance, role modeling, and to fast track you throughout your new assignment.

Take calculated risks and always move step by step

Whether you decide to drive your car over an icy road, or invest in a large sum of money in a new investment opportunity, there is a hidden chance of exposure to loss or injury. The difference here is that you will be encouraged to embrace such risk after its advantages and disadvantages have been carefully weighed and considered.

Concentrate more on the short term, and plan well to have strong starts and quick wins.

You'll gain nothing in the long term without determining your short-term plan and having its goals fully accomplished. If you've worked in sales like me, and had an annual target to achieve, you would know exactly what I mean. It is "January" sales - my friend- which you need to exceed comfortably to put you on the right track for achieving quarter one target and so on so forth. Otherwise, you'll taste the bitterness of being in a catch-up mode until the end of the quarter or most probably till the end of the year.

For myself, nothing motivates me like achievements, even if they are small ones. I insist on having them fast, with each initiative I go through. I plan and work massively to get them, not just to celebrate but to step on them to go up and up.

Move laterally when needed, and always diversify your wallet

When there is no obvious way to move up in your career, don't hesitate to move laterally to another department or company to have a new experience. It is always a smart tactical move that may open bigger future opportunities for you. Don't be stuck or shrink with the status quo. Instead, accept the move that will expose you to more contacts and responsibilities. Enjoy seeing the full picture of your organization or your industry. Enjoy a fresh start less off the pressure a promotion can bring. On the other hand, if you are investing you should refrain from putting all the eggs in one basket. Instead, create a safe and promising portfolio, then provide the right experience to design and manage this portfolio.

Tolerate transitions

Dr. Aml was a senior microbiology researcher at a leading national research center in her country when she had to leave "literally" everything and travel immediately to Turkey before the police force could come and arrest her. They had already arrested her husband, who had been protesting against the new military ruler who ousted the democratically elected president a few days ago. She traveled with her two little daughters to the "unknown," leaving two older children in the hands of some relatives. When I first saw her, she was looking sad yet constant, worried about how she could bring the two older kids and how she could find out about her husband, who was moving from one jail to another without yet having a trial. When I met her she asked me two questions which surprised me a bit. The first question was "Is the Turkish language easy to learn?" and the second was "Where do you think I can find a job in this city?" Istanbul, she meant. A few months later she told me that her husband had been sentenced to three years in jail, while she had been judged in absentia five years for protesting. But the good news was that she had succeeded in bringing her other two children to Istanbul. She told me that she was volunteering in some social activities while the kids went to school, and that they had all become good at the Turkish language. Three years after that, I learned that this lady is now teaching in one of the prominent Turkish universities, at the same time working as a consultant for one of the food factories in the city. The older two kids got a scholarship at the university, and her husband, who is an expert in the field of renewable energy, completed his sentence and is about to join the rest of the family.

Away from the big deal of persistence, perseverance, and love in the story of this woman, she demonstrated an amazing attitude dealing with the psychological dynamics of herself and her family during the transition period that followed a massive and painful change in their life. Can you imagine the amount of resistance and emotional upheaval that she and her kids felt when they were forced to let go of something that they were comfortable with back home? How much fear, anger, denial, frustration, and uncertainty they experienced as a result of the misfortune change which had happened in their life?

For each change, there is a corresponding transition. Thus you have to accept that something is ending before you can begin to accept the new idea. Of course, you'll most probably feel confused, uncertain, and impatient. You'll experience a higher workload as you get used to new systems and new ways of working. But the good news for you is that you are bridging an ending phase in your life to a new beginning, so don't panic when you feel such low morale, low productivity, and anxiety about what you are doing, or even about your status or identity. The last transition stage is a time of acceptance and energy.

Have the right attitude

As you face uncertainty, your brain habitually pushes you to panic. However, emotionally intelligent people can override this mechanism and shift their thinking in a rational direction. The brain loves knowing what's unknown. Thus smart people view obstacles as opportunities rather than threats. Having a positive attitude and maintaining a clear perspective is essential to overcoming uncertainties in life and business. Uncertain situations are mostly tough for you if you haven't been trained to expect them or if you haven't built the right mindset to face them. The following are four key practices that will help you to tolerate uncertainty in life and business:

Don't be panicked

When change happens in your life, and you start to become uncertain about its outcome, your brain reacts in a way that stimulates fear and anxiety at different levels. Fear and anxiety are two different feelings that often co-occur with uncertainty.

The unthinking reaction to uncertainty is fear, which happens as an emotional response to a known or definite threat, while anxiety comes from your mind's vision of the possible dangers that may result from the situation. This psychological state inhibits good decision-making process. People who have experience at resolving uncertainty are aware of this feeling, and spot it as soon as it begins to surface. A good tactic is to write down all that you fear because it could be subconsciously holding you back. Once you are aware of the fear, label all the irrational thoughts that try to intensify it as irrational fears, then you can focus more accurately and rationally on the information you have to go on.

Stay positive

In the face of uncertainty, you have to give your rambling brain a little help by consciously selecting something positive to think about. Anticipate happiness, health and success, and believe you can overcome any obstacle and difficulty, not just by saying this to yourself but by practicing positive thinking by a willingness to seek and explore new ideas. Assess a situation in an objective manner; look at the advantages and disadvantages. You need to be willing to make the appropriate adjustments. Moreover, always stay away from destructive thoughts and negative people, as studies have confirmed that negative emotions program your brain to do a specific action. Think positively but don't overstretch your mind; just remain balanced. Think more about favorable results and situations, but also expect the worst case scenario and be ready for it.

Let go of your obsession with goal-setting

It is muddy, drifting and cloudy; this is how your trail looks like throughout uncertain time and changes. So why insist on embracing strategic planning and long-term goal setting now? What you need more, I believe, is simple planning and step-by-step careful movement, as well as a big amount of faith, which should enable you to take calculated risk and move forward. On the other hand, don't play the game of expectations and lose your time in daydreaming. Instead of expecting the future to give you something specific, focus on what you'll do to create what you want to experience.

During uncertain situations and transitional times, I believe it is more important to focus on procedure and practice than the result or goals. When I quit my job and started up my own consultancy business, I was not thinking of certain specific objectives to reach as much as acquiring every day a new experience and improving my performance in areas such as creating attractive sales proposals, landing new clients, e-marketing, and many other critical things which I believed would make me confidently growing and successful. I did not forget my overall purpose, but I was focusing more on acquiring the right enablers, and enjoying the new experience.

Move forward

Do you know that during uncertain times, many people have a tendency to stick to memories? Either to blame themselves for certain decisions that, perhaps, are the reason for their life becoming tough, or living the nirvana of past victories and waiting until life flips again. The action is the antidote to fear. When life gets hard, keep moving forward one step at a time; it is the wisest thing to do. Admit the troubles that you are in, face your fear, look at the situation from a different angle, read a lot every day, branch out and learn from other people or organizations, give it a leap of faith, and just do it.

Learn from the birds

Birds leave early in the morning from their nests. They go hungry, nothing in their stomachs, but they return in the later part of the day with filled stomachs. Birds do this every day, everywhere on earth. Whatever the weather or the situation may be, they fly; they never question the certainty of going out that day. They just fly and do what they have to do, without expecting anything less than what God reserved for them. Those birds go out early in the morning to faraway places and then are guided to return to their proper places without erring. Truly a bird sitting in its nest will not have its stomach filled. It must go out and work hard. Birds, with their pure hearts teach you to live with satisfaction, abundance and to trust God, the one who is sufficient to take care of all matters. Their dynamic personality gets goals done and activities moving forward, just as you need to do.

CHAPTER 3

ALIGN WITH "CHANGE"

Since childhood, I have embraced many life changes. During my life, I have lived in four different countries in over 15 apartments, attended four public schools and two universities, and had about five different careers. In the last three years, my small children learned two new languages. Was it cool? Of course not! It was sometimes maddening, but I adapted to it and, with time, I learned how to deal with it in a different way than many others around me do. I could even say that I learned that not all the changes in our life are compulsory; some could be elective. Accordingly, I also learned when it is the right time to make a certain change in my life. I make changes when I no longer believe in the value of something, especially having experienced problems with it, at the same time I start lying to myself to avoid admitting the truth. I simply recognize that change is a constant in my life, and it is better for me to take it as a friend than an enemy that I must resist. Do you want to know why I consider change as my best friend? Because, change shows me my reality without any delusion while –sometimes- a stable life, routine job, and your loved ones might mask your reality. You will not be able to know your potential without embracing change and accepting the imminent challenges.

The moment of truth

When I immigrated to Canada, I struggled to find my first Canadian job after many years of a successful career back home; I had to ask myself every day what was it that I didn't know about myself that was making it so hard to find a job? I discovered a new answer every day, such as my English language, my networking capabilities, my adaptation skills, and so on. At that stage, my "personal development project" had been launched intensively under the pressure of the new change that had happened in my life. Without that change, I would remain under many false beliefs about myself. In the same way I became an entrepreneur in a new field as leaving my salary job to my first owned business was simply done due to accepting new life changes and rapidly adapting to it.

I always see change as my alarm that awakens me from under-performing or being just average in life. When change comes, it drives me to remember my life purpose, and makes me always want to stick more and more to my core values and life mission as a protective mechanism against the upcoming challenge and uncertainty.

Through all these changes in my life, I became more educated, talented, and strong. Having to travel to more than 15 different countries for doing business and networking helped me to learn different languages and become familiar with cross-cultural differences as well as religions, history and geography.

Change is always my growth catalyst. Each change is a turning point in my life; it is about closing one chapter and opening another one. Each change brings a new beginning and excitement to my life.

The Paradigm shift

As you can see, once you start looking at change as a good thing, you'll be amazed at some of the benefits that can follow. Embracing change is a real paradigm shift, which often involves re-evaluating your belief system.

There is hardly anything in life that is not changing. Changes are all around you; they are inevitable and constant; technology, education, health, eating habits, dress and everything. Some changes you may like, while others create fear and anxiety. For me, it would be easier to deal with changes if I had the answers to questions like: What am I going to do if such thing happens? How will my lifestyle be affected? What's in it for me? Having such answers can significantly reduce the worry about any potential change in my life, as the uncertainty about it is decreased. The secret in all that is in the way you view change, and to what extent you can deal with the accompanying uncertainty.

I have always asked myself if I want to be the person who can sail gently through the changes life throws at him, or to do like many others who get easily upset if they just have to change one of their daily routines. Most people don't choose to change; they prefer the security of what they know. Although we may intellectually know that things are changing and changing faster, the way we react is different. So if it doesn't feel like things are changing that much, you do not actively and strongly look for new ways to adapt to that change, but when you feel change is at your door, you start assessing its impact on three main areas which are your career, life quality, and relationships.

Can a period of high change be great for your life or career? My experience says that during such uncertain time if you do your job very well, you will shine while others around you fall apart at the seams. Your business will expand during the recession, and when circumstances get to be stable, you'll boom up.

Organizational change management

My involvement with organizational change started very early in my career, when I joined one of the growing family-owned health care companies as a marketing specialist. This company built its previous history in superior product quality and a strong sales machine. There was no 'real' marketing, HR, or customer service departments; the operation was mostly sales driven more than anything else, which was a big strategic risk, especially with the growing local and international competition. Accordingly, the company's leadership had no choice but to induce a massive organizational change management project in order to stay competitive in the market. The result was amazing; we became the market leader over five years, and even exceeded all the planned strategic objectives. Was it easy? Of course not. You might think that the major plight was the cost or the impact on productivity or knowledge; all these aspects were tough, but nothing was as devastating as managing the internal resistance among most of the staff.

So what was in it for me after all this? I got promoted twice during this period, first to a product manager position then to a business unit manager, with significant growth in my salary and benefits. After a while I got hunted by one of the biggest multinational companies to lead their healthcare business, at an increasingly higher level. Do you want to know why this happened to me while many others within the same organization, unfortunately, lost their jobs during that time? The answer was simply because I saw those staggering five years as an opportunity to learn and earn. I decided to be positive and fully engaged in the change process. I was planning ahead, self-organized, raising the bar on myself, and always motivated to see the great results.

Why do some people have a positive change management attitude and others don't? The answer, in my opinion, is because the first ones have a clear life purpose supported by strong values, and they are all the way committed to their personal success.

Leadership reactions to imminent changes

In business, leaders play a major role in determining the whole organization's future through the way they look to the upcoming changes in technology or other market factors. They might decide to lead the change or manage to stay and improve through adaptation with the looming change, or in many cases get trapped in denial and avoidance until being a victim of this change. Below are three stories that explain the three different situations:

Leading the changes through innovation

I still remember when I joined 3M Company in 2007 as a business leader. I was curious to understand how such a huge diversified business --with more than 50,000 products, and 70,000 employees in more than 200 different working locations all over the world -- was working so smoothly. But the more interesting thing to me was how, after more than a century in business, such an old company could stay innovative and not run out of fresh ideas. I discovered the answer when I realized that, from the chief executive on down, the company was committed to innovation.

3M was awarded the US government's highest award for innovation, the National Medal of Technology. Over a 20-year period, 3M's gross margin averaged 51%, and the company's return on assets averaged 29%. 3M has consistently been highly ranked, often in the top 20, in Fortune magazine's annual survey of "America's Most Admired Corporations."

The reason behind this massive success story is the innovation mindset and leadership strategy of reinventing the company every few years.

The power of adaptation to looming change

Adaptation in business is not far away from adaptation in biology. It is a method to stay vital through improvement. It usually includes intense structural modification, product development and other strategies that drive functional improvement.

DuPont is a good example of a company that has adapted over time. Now known as one of the world's largest chemical companies, DuPont got its start in gunpowder. From its origins in explosives, DuPont ultimately added other businesses like lacquers and synthetic rubber before inventing the first polyesters, nylon, Teflon and the first phenothiazine insecticide. Along the way, the company continued to pioneer new plastics and synthetics, but also products in fields such as crop science (seeds and fertilizers), healthcare, electronics, and nutrition.

The tragedy of change avoidance

Nowadays, when I see the real "mania" of taking "selfie" photos among all generations, and when I think of the millions of digital photos pushed every single hour from all over the globe into billions of social media accounts, I believe more and more in the human instinct of capturing the moment. Kodak's tragedy started to happen when it focused more on the product which was the "film" instead of looking at the real customer value which was the ability to capture the moment.

Due to Kodak management's inability to see digital photography as a disruptive technology, and to move into the digital world quickly enough, Kodak filed for bankruptcy protection in 2012, exited legacy businesses and sold off its patents before re-emerging as a much smaller company in 2013. Once one of the most powerful companies in the world, today the company has a market capitalization of less than $1 billion.

Retirement as a life change

Is retirement one of the "worrying" future changes that you are expecting? If so, what did you do to prepare for it? Do you know that a large percentage of older working forces all over the developed countries are heading into retirement without adequate savings to keep them out of poverty? A new study suggests that half of Canadian couples between 55 and 64 have no employer pension between them, and of those, less than 20 percent of middle-income families have saved enough to adequately supplement government income.

What is your insurance, saving or investment plan? What is your strategy to avoid being broke at that critical age? Obviously, a good way to deal with such life change is to be always proactive, because this makes you feel more in control. And the more you feel you have control over the situation, the less stress and frustration you feel.

You need to think of a strategic move, which -by the way- will change your lifestyle starting from now, to avoid "painful" changes at the age of retirement. You may need to change your spending habits and start saving some money, not waiting until a later that never comes. You need to stop looking at your credit card debt as a fact of life. In addition you may need to revisit your plans for financing any depreciated assets and prepare yourself to sell a certain asset which you own upon retirement and so on so forth. Start from now to be ready by having the right mindset and taking smart actions, which can take you to your dream retirement, and reduce your uncertainty about your future.

Your best ally

How can you make "change" your best ally that catalyzes your growth and success in life and business? The answer is that you need to deal with "change" as a process that starts from within and encompasses some logical and collaborative steps. You need first to be aware of the current situation, and know where you want to reach then. For example, if you decide to quit your job to be an entrepreneur, it is important to be aware of many things like the amount of effort and risk included in such a move. In the same way, you should be fully aware of the time and resources needed to reach where you want to reach. Then you need to have the needed knowledge about the type of product, service or idea that can fit a real market need and generate profit, the needed legal framework to protect your business, the industry rule and regulations, the market and of course the competition.

Furthermore, you need to make sure that you have the necessary competence, talent, skills, and aptitude to practice what you know, and to use your knowledge in a professional manner, in order to achieve business results and gain experience.

Finally, before you quit your job and start up your own business, you need to provide some measures to guarantee a smooth transition and safe operation in your first years. You can do that -for example-by working part-time in your current job before quitting completely. You may consider having the right coach, mentor or partner in your field who helps you oversee obstacles in your way and advises you how to overcome them quickly. Such measures help to avoid any possible backsliding to the undesired status which initially called for change. When dealing with any change in your personal or business life, the above-explained way of preparing and dealing with change will help you to overcome many potential gaps and threats.

CHAPTER 4

THE DESIRED LEADERSHIP

When I was a business leader for one of the top global diversified technology companies, I went through many uncertain situations which were tough enough to make any leadership question the value of continuing to run the business in such conditions! One of these situations was during the global financial crisis of 2007-2008; the region was the Middle East with that well-known amount of political and economic volatility! The global financial crisis came out on top. It was not the first time, and it will not be the last!

I watched some local and international companies collapse, or minimized their operations around the world, but that was not the case with my company. I was exceeding my operational plans, the whole company was expanding around the world through acquiring other companies like never before, and the growth in sales and profit was really great.

This company had been chosen as the year's best company in the Leaders survey conducted by management consultancy *Hay Group* and *Chief Executive Magazine*. In that uncertain time, my organization was not pulling back on its development of leaders, but instead made serious investments in leadership development. What we achieved was not only due to the innovative products or the surplus cash that we had, although those were a great support; the main reason, in my opinion, was that we were ready!

As a leader in this organization, I was trained on how to master uncertainty, so I knew exactly what I should do and I got the right enablers which allowed me to pass the dark tunnel safely and successfully. So, what is the golden leadership rule that you need to have in order to create the success you want, especially during uncertain times? The answer, in my opinion, is you have to lead yourself perfectly while leading the transformation itself.

Lead yourself first!

The first thing you need to lead perfectly is yourself, through what I call the personal leadership approach. It implies to demonstrate effective governance to each of your life's four major domains, which are:

- Your personal life
- Your career
- Your family
- Your community

Actually, inside each of these main areas are many topics and concerns so to lead through this concept, you need first to determine what are these issues which you need to focus on within each of your different life domains.

For example, you might put under "Personal life" something like your health, education, spirituality, relationships, and hopes. For your "Career" you may think of things like performance, income, training, promotion, business development, and networking. For your "Family" domain you might consider things related to your nuclear family or your extended one. For the "Community" domain, which is, unfortunately, less considered by many of us, you might think of some philanthropic, social, or political responsibilities.

Now you need to set your strategic goals in each different area of your life, and effectively develop your life vision, which should represent your ultimate success in life for the long term. While doing this make sure to recognize then eliminate any possible conflict within your different life domains tasks, as they should be compatible and work in harmony to achieve your life vision. For example, if you have in your career objectives "to be an entrepreneur" it would be logical to find something like "being rich and financially free" within your personal domain objectives. At the same time, it could shape your friendship style and have a reflection on the way you are supporting your community, and so on. What is important now, when you deal with these four life domains concept, is that you need to apply a set of four principles to guarantee the maximum benefit of this concept. Those principles are:

Principle one: It has to be all inclusive

Meaning you should think and work on all the four life domains; the personal, the career, the family and the community, not neglecting or underestimating the importance of any of them. It is a package deal.

Principle two: It has to be all balanced

While executing your mission in each of your four life domains, you need to keep the balance between all of them. No bias or favoritism. Such "unwanted" bias sometimes manifested in cases such as where a woman is spending 90% of her time taking care of her family without paying attention to her personal life, or a man who has fully dedicated himself to his job with no time or energy for his family. In such cases, she or he would certainly need to know how to rebalance their life!

But it is worth it to say that, in some life stages or conditions, it is normal to have that type of imbalance, due to certain specific circumstances as what could happen when you have just left your job and started your own business. Or if you are a student who is preparing for final exams. Or you are a new mother, etc. In such situations, the bottom line is:

- There should be a strong reason for such imbalance to take place.
- It should not stay for a long time as you have to rebalance your life in the nearest possible time after resolving your emergencies!

Principle three: It should be deep

So, don't expect this model to work, or to be productive by serving each life domain task in a superficial way; you need to dig deep in each aspect to reach your objectives and always remember it is a whole life management approach. For example, if supporting kids with special needs is one of your community domain tasks that you want to do it successfully so you need to dig deep into the concept of community support especially children with special needs, and you need to know the guidelines, best practices, and who has the knowledge, etc.

Simply make yourself deeply trained and educated about what you want to pursue. This is valid for each of your different life domains tasks.

Principle Four: It should be scientifically correct

For example, if you have children and raising them with good psychological and physical health is one of your family domain missions, but your way to do this is by just following some common or traditional advice which you hear here and there, I'm not sure that this will help you be successful. I believe that you have to follow the correct, updated, scientifically based guidelines and experiences related to such matter.

If you can reach this level of self-insight and control, you'll be more excellent in managing your life priorities, and this will help you accomplish your mission in life. You will be able to lead by example, and change others' lives while you are positively changing yourself.

Lead the transformation

In a world that is rapidly changing, you need to adapt quickly to meet the requirements of the changing environment. The organization which you lead regardless its size and mission have a big chance to remain successful and competitive in the long term if you adapt the transformational leadership concept. It is all about creating valuable and positive change within your followers, with the end goal of developing them into leaders.

You as a leader should dedicate yourself to inspire individuals, develop trust, and encourage creativity and personal growth, while individuals should work to develop a sense of purpose to benefit the group, organization, or society. This should go beyond their own self-interests and an exchange of rewards or recognition for effort or loyalty. To achieve this you need to:

Be the role model

You need to provide a role model for high ethical behavior, instilling pride, and gaining respect and trust. *Mahatma Gandhi* and *Nelson Mandela* are classical models for transformational leaders who made themselves a real living model of what they called for.

If you are a father or a mother, you are in a leadership position where practicing such things as healthy living, self-Improvement, volunteering, self-control, and a positive attitude will make you a powerful role model for your children. Whatever your leadership position in life, walking your talk and leading by example is your magic way to credibility and influence.

Inspire confidence through articulating a vision that is appealing and inspiring to your people

Leaders with inspirational motivation challenge followers with high standards, communicate optimism about future goals, and provide meaning for the task at hand. Do you believe that massive thoughts need massive actions? If so, determine the right estimation for the work needed, communicate it in a positive way, and never reduce the target.

Juliette Gordon Low, the founder of the Girl Scouts Movement, before women had the right to vote in the USA, Juliette had a vision of a movement that would be exclusively for girls, and through her dedication, dynamism, and tenacity, she inspired others to make her vision a reality.

Think big and have amazing, inspiring communication with your people, focus on the strength of all and do whatever it takes to make them reach places they would not normally go by themselves.

Be creative by challenging assumptions, taking risks and solicit your team's ideas

With this style, you stimulate and encourage creativity in your people.

Steve Jobs, co-founder of Apple, focused on creating the next attractive products of his company. He released the iMac, the iPod, iTunes and the iPhone, and restored Apple's image. The

creative leadership of *Jobs* made Apple stock rise like never.
Another story is about the LEGO bricks. If all LEGO offered was a box of bricks, there would be many other companies out there who would counterfeit that and sell it for a lower price.

But the company became very adept at developing not just boxes of bricks, but boxes of bricks with stories and games attached to them. The result was extreme growth in the company's sales, profit, and brand recognition.

Nowadays many world leaders believe that **managing despite uncertainty will require a lot of creativity.** At one side, creativity is needed to make decisions quickly and soundly. While at the other, only creative leaders have the ability to re-think their strategies or business models and come up with ideas to drastically change their organizations.

Motivate individually by attending to each follower's needs

Act as a mentor or coach to your team members. Listen to their concerns and needs and always make sure that you regularly:

- Express words of thanks or praise as a means of motivation
- Make public recognition of achievements and initiatives
- Write private notes of congratulations to boost self-confidence
- Ensure fair workload distribution
- Take individualized career counseling and mentoring

Whether you are a project manager or a soccer team captain, you need to know that motivating both individual members and the team as whole is important to achieve your organizational objectives.

Meantime as a leader you should not to be confused about the difference between motivation and incentive. Incentive is "I am going to pay you to want what I want." As a mother or father, if you pay your child to want what you want, they do it. The minute you stop paying them, they stop. And they are not motivated to do anything. In contrast, motivation is an engine inside of you. You are committed to doing what you should do, whether you are paid or not. You always need to give empathy and support in a genuine way, and to be sensitive to the individual variations among your team when deciding your motivation actions. If you want to be a real leader you must know that managing uncertainty is a matter of putting yourself in the shoes of your people and delivering the compassionate leadership they expect.

Last but not least, during life and business insecurity, people don't want to hear good wishes from their leaders; they want their leaders to be strong, confident, decisive, fully transparent and dedicated to the success and wellbeing of all.

CHAPTER 5

STAY SHARPLY FOCUSED

During times of uncertainty, there is nothing more important to focus on than focusing on "you". You should be more mindful of the way you are consuming your attention, energy and time. You should learn how to pick your battles and make your decisions. When making decisions, both the rational and emotional parts of your brain are active. Sometimes overwhelming emotions like fear and anxiety which usually associate with uncertainty can cloud your judgment when you must make important decisions. Certain situations may require more activity in the rational part of your brain, while others will require more activity in the emotional part. These two sections are always competing, and typically you are equipped to call upon either section to help you with your decisions.

Generally speaking, your brain is hardwired to make much of modern life difficult. Therefore when you face uncertainty, your brain sometimes pushes you to overreact. Successful people can override this mechanism and shift their thinking in a more rational direction. You have the power to steer your own course through uncertainty. All you need is to stay sharply focused.

Focus on the value of time

Time is not money; time is your life. You can make money, but you can't make time. If you lost money you could compensate for it, but can you compensate for lost time? It is your responsibility to use your time wisely. The uncertainty about life and business is mostly overwhelming unorganized people, who have poor control over their day and consequently their whole life. You can say that much of your life is driven by someone else's agenda or outside pressures, things you have to do, things you would like to do, things you are expected to do. But where could all these beliefs take you? My simple answer is; they will take you to increasingly suffering until you break down eventually.

Accordingly, you need to stand up and have the precise focus, and think how you can get the maximum value of every single day of your life. In other words, how can you add quality to every single day of your life? My experience in doing this came through a simple rule which is; finding connections between time and values. Thus, whatever you value more in life, either being money, health, spirituality, or power, you should prioritize your daily tasks accordingly. So you give them more time, energy, and dedication. By the end of the day you will feel much more satisfied and fulfilled, and your quality of life will improve accordingly.

Now you are focusing on what is adding life to your days more than anything else. Meanwhile, be always aware and alert to what is called "time thieves." There are many of them in your today's life, among the most dangerous ones of which is "failure to set goals in life." This is your biggest resource drainer in my opinion, which is capable, alone of causing you to always feel uncertain, lost and broke.

Another dangerous time thief is "procrastination," which is the act or habit of delaying or putting off something that requires immediate attention. There are many examples in your life, like delaying responding to job emails or calling back someone; even doing your laundry or paying your bills at the time. Regardless of how smart you are, if you constantly procrastinate, this will lead you to be late with your assignments, and you might lose your job or any opportunity. Hence cut off procrastination; just do it and never break a deadline, as by doing this you are losing not only your time but in many cases someone else's time as well. At the same time, you need to realize that "too much socialization," especially at the workplace, leads to procrastination. Examples include excessive chatting, unnecessary personal phone calls, unauthorized or extended breaks, non-work related social media involvement, etc.

Accommodate to have the right vision

Just as when your eye changes its optical power to maintain a clear image or focus on an object as its distance varies, you need to train your brain to accommodate similarly, aiming to have the clearest possible vision during uncertain times.

In business, traditional industry reports, indirect market feedback or secondary data might not reflect the real image about a business situation, especially during uncertain periods. Accordingly, your future projection will not be accurate.

A good thing to do in such situations is to collect first-hand information from the field. Meet the business stakeholders and listen to them carefully. Take your notes, get the freshest and most accurate data about your targets, analyze deeply, and do some cross-checking for the data you have received, by using different reality checking techniques.

Conduct Voice of the Customer surveys to acquire an in-depth understanding of your customers' and prospects' preferences and actions. Simply put down your glasses and train your eyes to see distantly without them. And remember the more light that lands on your target, the easier it is to see. Just as when you step outdoors into direct sunlight, your natural vision can improve dramatically.

In today's world, information is abundant to the level that exceeds our capacities to digest it. If the information you have is massive but irrelevant or inaccurate or outdated, this will not help you make the right decision or build a winning strategy. This will just increase your uncertainty. You need to have a system that allows you to focus exactly on what you need, and makes it easy for you to process the available data and make the best use of it. People who have problems seeing distance with their eyes know that very well, as they face it when the distorting lights come from everywhere and make it difficult for them to focus on their target. In such situations they aim to block out light rays coming from all different angles, only allowing light rays to enter the eye head-on. This makes the inner lens no longer needed to precisely focus, and refracts light rays to create a clear vision so they can see better. It is the same in your life and business as you must be specific when it comes to your strategic goals; tune and tune again until you get focused, have your lens shuttering mechanism set to avoid the haziness coming from excessive inputs, so you can see your destination clearly.

Learn from Eisenhower

Dwight Eisenhower was the 34th President of the United States, serving two terms from 1953 to 1961. During his time in office, he launched programs that directly led to the development of the Interstate Highway System in the United States, the launch of the internet (DARPA), the exploration of space (NASA), and the peaceful use of alternative energy sources (Atomic Energy Act). Before becoming president, Eisenhower was a five-star general in the United States Army and served as the Supreme Commander of the Allied Forces in Europe during World War II. At other points along the way, he served as President of Columbia University, became the first Supreme Commander of NATO, and somehow found time to pursue hobbies like golfing and oil painting. He lived one of the most productive lives you can imagine. He once related his life to his effective strategy in dealing with tasks and setting priorities. This strategy has become famous as the *Eisenhower Matrix*, also referred to as *Urgent-Important Matrix* which could help you prioritize tasks according to their urgency and importance, sorting out less urgent and important tasks which you should either delegate or not do at all. The following techniques will help you implement this amazing life management philosophy within different time ranges, from a single day up to many years.

- Putting things-to-do on a list to free-up your mind and always question what is worth doing first.
- Try limiting yourself to no more than eight tasks per quadrant. Before adding another task, complete the most important one first. Remember: It is not about collecting but about finishing tasks.
- You should always maintain only one list for both business and private tasks. That way you will never be able to complain about not having done anything for your family or yourself at the end of the day.
- Do not let yourself or others distract you. Do not let others define your priority. Plan in the morning then work on your stuff. And in the end, enjoy the feeling of completion.
- Finally, try not to procrastinate that much. Not even by over-managing your to-dos.

Hit the sweet spot

If you have ever played tennis, most likely you know about the "sweet spot." It's that preferred spot where the racquet hits the ball and it feels good, as you're in maximum control of the ball, and that makes you incredibly thrilled. If the ball impacts at a point well away from the sweet spot, you will feel jarring and vibration of the racquet handle; it doesn't feel right, and you spend more effort with less possibility to score.

In your life, the sweet spot is the slight intersection between two important imaginary circles in your life. The first circle includes subjects that really matter in your life, such as your health, faith, career, prosperity, relationships, self-respect, etc.

The second circle contains things that you can control, such as your attitudes, beliefs, daily habits, the way you spend money, your friends, your thoughts, etc.

You need to check to which extent you are concerned and consumed with things that are not really of great importance to you, meaning not significantly contributing to your life mission and not adding any quality to your life. These things can make you unhappy and unsatisfied. In the same way, you need to think of those things you can't do anything about, as they are not fully under your span of control. For example, what people say or think about you, natural disasters, weather, traffic, and the past or future events.

When you do this exercise, you'll be surprised that things that do matter in your life are few. Likewise, you'll find the things that you can control.

Accordingly, the most important thing you should start doing immediately in your life is to focus sharply on the "very very" few things that significantly matter to you and at the same time are under your control.

In business and career, the same concept is applied. So if you are an employee who is working for an organization, you need to concentrate on the intersecting area between three different circles of purpose which are your organizational purpose, your own personal purpose, and your specific role purpose. If all three can come to overlap, the positive interconnection between the three distinct definitions of purpose should be your career sweet spot that usually felt by yourself, your team, the organization, customers, and perhaps most importantly, society as a whole.

In the same way, if you are doing business, you can look with strategic focus into the very specific area where your company's offer meets significant, quantified customer needs, away from what the competition is offering. That is your business' sweet spot, and that is where your profits skyrocket.

But what if you are uncertain about what career opportunities you might want to pursue, or what your ideal role is in your life? In that case, you need to build your vision through answering three important questions. First, what is that I'm extremely passionate about? Second, what do I believe I'm good at or can be best at? Third, what do other people value, that I can make money doing? If you have clear and candid answers for these three interrelated questions, you will uncover another sweet spot in your life, which is the intersecting area between your passion, abilities, and opportunities. If you concentrate your focus on this area, your chances to determine the most matching career or role for you in life will be higher and that consequently should reduce your uncertainty about the future.

Enhance Relationships

In my opinion, one of the best parts of being human is being able to connect with other humans. We're hardwired for it. God had created us from a male and a female, and made the whole of humanity into nations and tribes, so that we may know one another. We live in groups and families, work in teams, love as couples and thrive in friendships. The drive to connect is within you, whether you acknowledge it or not.

With uncertainty about the future, focusing on keeping, developing and leveraging relationships is a true wisdom and a golden key for a long life of happiness. One strong proof of this idea is what is known as the *Harvard Grant Study,* a 75-year longitudinal Grant and Glueck study led by *George Vaillant* and *Sheldon Glueck.* The eminent study has found "strong relationships" to be far and away the strongest predictor of life satisfaction. And regarding career satisfaction, too, feeling connected to one's work was far more important than making money or achieving traditional success.

I believe that the second most important relationship in your life, after your relationship with your God, is the relationship with your parents. If one or both attain old age in your life, you should be very sensitive to what you say to them, and address them with honor. Be dutiful, respectful and always available for them.

If you do have children, enjoy being there for them. Instead of just ignoring your children and letting them get on with life alone, help them up when they fall. Listen to them. Tell your children you love them every day, no matter what their age is. Go into their rooms at nighttime and read them a bedtime story. Let them fall asleep to the sound of your voice. Have a walk around the neighborhood with each of your children as a kind of one-on-one opportunity. Assist them if they need help with their homework, don't just tell them to ask a sibling. They want you to help them.

With your friends; be a good friend, one who lets his friends have total freedom to be themselves. That's what real friendship amounts to -- letting a person be who he really is.

I believe that whatever your style is, or whatever kind of relationship you want to embrace, there are common essentials required to have it work well. One of the essentials for good relationship building is to be open-minded for new people and ideas. So regardless of who is on the other part of the relationship, you must listen to their opinions and respect them. Also, you need to provide the needed time for the relationship, whether it is to meet or have a chat, etc.

I believe that to have good relationships with others, you should never ignore people who really care for you. Away from your many responsibilities and tight schedule, try to find an occasion or a method to communicate your feelings or attitude towards a caring person; don't ignore her or him and don't hurt her or his feelings. Truthfully, Focusing on the genuine and healthy relationship could be your winning strategy to pursue happiness in your life.

Stop Multi-tasking

Browsing the web while eating your breakfast, texting while walking, sending emails during meetings, chatting on the phone while cooking dinner. Sound familiar? In today's life, doing just one thing at a time seems like a rare luxury. You have become a master of multi-tasking.

When multi-tasking is the norm, your brain quickly adapts so you lose the ability to focus as distraction becomes a habit. We've trained our brains to be unfocused. Many recent studies have found that constant multi-tasking may be hindering your performance. My personal experience with the habit of multi-tasking tells me that it sometimes can increase your efficiency and allow you more time at the end of the day to do the things you love, but this is not a rule; it is very situational and differs from one person to another. In brief, I see multi-tasking as just a bad habit some people got addicted to.

With multi-tasking maybe you can accomplish a lot more by doing two or more things at once, but what does the finished product looks like? What will the quality and reliability is of what you are producing or offering? When people in the workplace are handling more than one job task at the same time, it is slowing them down, not the opposite. In fact, it will probably take them longer to finish two assignments when they are jumping back and forth than it would to finish each one separately.

The most annoying aspect of multi-tasking, from my point of view, is that it can steal the enjoyment of the moment. Multi-tasking tends to dilute the feeling of pleasure that you can have if you just do things one by one. Think of dining, reading, listening to music, or being in a lecture, with multi-tasking you lose the needed relaxation to recharge your battery for the upcoming working day.

According to the American Psychological Association's overview of multi-tasking research, only 2% of the population is actually proficient at multi-tasking. In general, having the right focus on accomplishing tasks one by one rather than multi-tasking will help you to be more efficient and effective, and making this a habit will make your life more organized and joyful.

On the whole; not all things in your life are worth your full attention; you need to focus sharply on what really matters, and at the same time, what you can control. Don't care too much about what happened to you in the past. Instead, focus on what is coming next. Give your full attention to things you can't compensate for if they get lost, such as your time, health, and relationships. Be sure to focus more on your strategic objectives, which are in nature highly vital yet less urgent. This is your golden key to lead and prosper.

Live each day of your life with a great sense of gratitude and hope, and always focus on how you can pursue happiness through healthy, sustainable and balanced relationships.

CHAPTER 6

RETHINK YOUR LIFE STRATEGY

Are you constantly thinking about how to create value or how to strengthen your position in the face of uncertainty and invent a new future for yourself and the people around you? Are you trying to find innovative ways of doing things to replace old, outdated ones? If your answers to these questions are yes, then welcome to the club of brave game changers!

Your life approach is particularly designed for your beliefs, values, and decisions about using your time, energy, money, skills and other resources. That is what crafts your life plan. In fact traditional ways to planning for your life can be dangerous, as they may lead you to view uncertainty in a binary way, meaning, to assume that the world is either certain, and therefore open to accurate predictions or uncertain, and therefore completely unpredictable.

I believe it is not the matter of under- or over-estimating uncertainty in your life or business, as much as it is your ability to make the right move before the "threat" hits you or the "opportunity" disappears. You have to learn how to discover the critical factors in a certain situation, and design a way to focus and coordinate your actions to manage accordingly.

When your future is complex and fast changing, your processes for preparing for it have to be, too. Thus you need to implement a customized and adaptive action planning process that should enable you to respond to these changes in logical and productive ways. But without having the right mind-set nothing will work. The following is a gear-shifting approach that should help you develop the needed attitude to change your life strategy in order to cope with the looming uncertainty, as you shift gears:

1. From expectations to actions

Instead of expecting the future to give you something in specific, work your plan to build the certainty you want to live. Your belief about what might happen in the future, alone, doesn't make it real. It is the realistic planning and serious implementation that paint your map for the foreseen future.

If success is what you want, then you need first to define this success by asking yourself what does it mean exactly to be successful? Secondly, you need to understand your enablers and constraints, then build on your strengths to reach where you want to be. Set goals but don't be so much obsessed with them. Instead focus more on the best use of the available resources and tools to develop your strategic competencies. Always raise the bar and exceed your initial goals.

Another thing to be aware of about expectations is that, when you make expectations, you may be setting yourself up for disappointment as you can't control the exact outcome. However, it might also be true that you will receive what you expect.

A real situation was documented in *Psychology Today* where a young man who had "A" grades through high school received a 98 on his SAT. He mistakenly thought it was his IQ and ended up almost failing his first year of college. When informed about the difference, he went back to being an "A" student. So be careful when you set your expectations, especially during uncertain times. And more importantly, work hard to shift your expectation towards the most positive outcome.

2. From rigidity to agility

If you are an old soccer fan like me, you may remember the old days when smart talented strikers were always subject to censorship by tall strong defenders who could turn their life into real misery just by staying close in order to inhibit them from receiving the ball comfortably. They simply used to disarme them, and this sometimes resulted in injuring the strikers. What those forwarders used to do in the past is escaping this close censorship by going back to the midfield aiming to freely receive some passes and start an attack from near of the midfield. By doing so, they were doing nothing except what the opponent defense wanted. Your opponent's wish is to push you away from the target area, and exhaust you each time you want to invade their side.

Fortunately, years ago, sports experts started to develop and implement new training programs aimed at increasing players' agility, meaning increasing the ability of the players to change the direction of their body abruptly or to shift the direction of movement quickly without losing balances. This attribute tremendously elevated the potential of the players, especially strikers, and allowed them to often beat the tough defenders, who were also agile but not skillful as some strikers and midfielders were. This overall concept makes the game more offensive and exciting.

Do you see any link with this concept and your fight to win different life challenges? And avoid life risks? The demands of high-performance agility in life are like in the sport; they inquire that you effectively deploy a blend of factors such as speed, strength, balance, and co-ordination. Likewise is the business in today's uncertain times. As recent Accenture research has identified leaders and laggards among companies around the world, regarding agility across five dimensions, from the speed of decision-making to knowing what is strategic and what is operational, to investing in and using analytics to leadership diversity, and finally having an ecosystem to act quickly.

3. From long-term to short-term

When I joined the school of medicine, I was aiming to graduate as a medical doctor after seven years. That was my long-term goal. My short-term goal was to achieve an "A" in a monthly MCQ quiz. I still remember one older alumni's advice to me was to not underestimate those frequent quizzes as they would affect my total GPA and would help me to obtain a scholarship available to highly achieving students, and in addition, would determine the early impressions of my teachers and other students around me. He was right, as doing well in the short-term will without a doubt, make the long-term objectives easily attainable and vice versa.

Short-term goals are like ladders to any ultimate goal you may want to reach, whether it's to purchase the needed food for a dinner party or to have your proficiency license in a year. Every step counts to reach your destination. And definitely, what time frame you set for your goals should be determined by what outcomes you are seeking.

With future uncertainty, long-term planning becomes difficult especially when you can't use the past to well predict the future. Long-term goals, milestones, task lists, and solid assumptions can't make any perfect sense. Instead you need to customize your plan based on your priorities after gathering intelligence about your environment and establishing simple rules, procedures and expectations to support implementation. Then you need to work hard to create a quick wins then step on them to reach the next level, until you can see better and formulate longer-term objectives based on what you had already accomplished. All the way stay adherent to your life purpose as this should enhance your progress through difficulties.

4. From top-line to bottom-line

In business, the bottom line refers to a company's net earnings, net income or profit. The reference to "bottom" describes the relative location of the net income value on a company's income statement. For sure you don't want to be like the business man who is overly focused on increasing his sales without regard to his costs.

This reminds me with the story of the Egyptian soccer team who had qualified only twice for the FIFA world cup, It played once in its life against Brazil, the team wich won this cup 5 times before. What happened that night is that the Egyptian team succeeded to score 3 truly amazing goals in Brazil but lost 3-4 at the very end of the match!! Brazil won the cup, and the Egyptian team went back home with exciting memories about scoring many goals in Brazil's net!

Most enterprises aim to improve their bottom line through two methods: growing revenues, i.e., generating top-line growth, and increasing efficiency or cutting costs. You can increase your sales to raise your net income, but this could be limited by factors like; competition or production capacity. Also, you can increase your profit by reducing cost. But this can work within certain limits as this might hurt the quality at longer term. Actually, there is a more effective way to increase your profit than just reducing cost, or increasing revenues. This occurs by improving your operation management. Operational excellence is achieved when you improve things like the processes by which goods and services are produced, the quality of goods or services, the inventory needed to produce goods or services, and the human resource management.

This philosophy can generally be applied in your life, by not taking it as a fight to maximize your income or minimize your expense. It is more your ability to use your resources wisely and economically, leverage your talents and increase your competitiveness. It is also by operating your life with good health, mindfulness, sound decisions, involvement, and positive relationships.

5. From solidity to liquidity

The most important thing that you need to learn during uncertainty is how to "untie" your bonds with traditional ways of doing things. As things are moving fast in an unpredictable manner, from ideology to workplaces and from technology to relationships you need to reduce your commitments for "unnecessary obligations" as this will let you sail smoothly through transitions without many life obligations.

For any person who lives in today's society, having bonds with others is a good thing, as long as it is not too firm and tight, simply because the uncertainty surrounding you will take you away from many traditional commitments. In the last few years, even, my 70-year-old mother has untightened many traditional bonds with places, persons, and methods of doing things to adapt to her new changing life. But she always surprises me by her style of keeping room for potential restoration of such relations at a possible future time. During uncertainty, your main challenge is to keep yourself relevant to the new situation more than constricting yourself to traditional bonds. As a human, you are not permanent, so don't seek permanence in anything.

In face of underlining uncertainty, liquidity turns out to be essential to avoid "calcification" and paralysis in relations and positions. With this in mind, you have to enhance your capability to establish and leverage a social network that can partially contribute to your success without over controlling your life especially during uncertain situations and transitions. It is not just the online network model which I mean; but also where you live, work, volunteer, play and have your meals.

The best networking style, in my opinion, is the one where everybody is keen to add value mutually and is likely to use it over time yet not forming solid boundaries around its members. You need to consider being part of a smart network, as who you surround yourself with will shape you in one way or another and will affect how you think and act in life. Indeed, your active network is an indicator of your life purpose.

You live and socially connect with others in a very small world, where the possibility to reconnect in the future is high, regardless of who you are or where you exist. It seems that you can't get lost in this super-connected world where there are more than 1.5 billion people monthly using Facebook, 400 million people monthly using Instagram, 320 million people monthly using Twitter, 300 million people monthly using Google+ and about 100 million people monthly using LinkedIn. Social media has created a chance for more liquid relations, which are easy to be established, maintained, blocked and reconnected.

Either online or offline, you need to make sure that your network is leveraging your capabilities to be successful and happy in life as people around you offer encouragement and support, challenge you to think big, and make the uncertainty around you less.

6. From judgment to self-awareness

With uncertain situations, I have noticed that many people are obsessed with judging two things: first, other people, on what they say or do, and second, judging what hasn't happened yet, or tomorrow which hasn't yet come! This happens mostly due to the fear and anxiety associated with uncertainty. The hardships that are usually associated with transitions and life changes might also make you lose the happiness of the current moment or the essence of a relationship you are currently in. The opposite seems to happen if you shift your concentration to yourself more than others, and try to opt for what is good for here and now. It is a good way to cope with uncertainty, as it makes you keener and more compassionate.

Moreover, spirituality and meditation help you to increase your self-awareness, as they act as a key to reconnecting with your true self. You gain many benefits from being aware of yourself as you become more self-disciplined, optimistic, emotionally intelligent and generally positive. Self-awareness, also, increases your decision-making abilities and helps you to keep cool and calm all the time.

Learning to be mindful and self-aware is something similar to learning how to drive a car. You should observe how you simultaneously watch the road, your car, and your body movements. Driving cars can't be learned only from books. You need to pay attention and stay alerted to every action or reaction on your way. The same is true of self-awareness, which by definition is what you develop when you pay attention to your expressions of thoughts, emotions, and behaviours.

For this reason, I adapted myself since long time to write every night before going to bed, about things I did during the day which made me happy and felt good, things that brought me closer to my dreams, and people for whom I felt grateful. This helped me to have a clearer perception of my personality, including strengths, weaknesses, thoughts, beliefs, motivation, and emotions. Self-observation helps you to understand how other people perceive you.

In sum, having self-awareness is a vital first step toward maximizing your uncertainty management skills. Self-awareness can improve your judgment and help you identify opportunities for professional development and personal growth.

7. From maximization to optimization

The rising uncertainty and imminent changes around you imply alert planning for your business, and may be a less adventurous lifestyle. Thus, you need to differentiate between what is essential and what is just nice to have. You don't want to carry-on in life with financial liabilities, but on the contrary you need fewer obligations and useful relationships. Instead of spreading yourself too thin, you need to think more of optimization rather than maximization. Optimization means looking for the best, while maximization means looking for the most. They are not the same.

An example of this is diversification of stock holdings. Studies have shown that the optimum number is ten (assuming they are truly diverse and not ten banks, for example). After you have ten holdings, adding another one doesn't improve results much, but rather, it just increases paperwork.

You may need to revisit your life goals, redefine your business objective and your whole lifestyle to make sure that you are working to reach your goals by satisfying certain mandatory constraints such as ethics, legal, and social constraints.

In sum, avoid excess. Live your life with gratitude and balance. Evade overabundance in everything, as even good things, attained without restraint, can convert to a source of trouble and suffering.

CHAPTER 7

TAKE RISK

Have you ever noticed that you often use the terms "risk" and "uncertainty" in the same way? In fact, both concepts are closely related but not the same. With risk, you don't know what is going to happen next, but you do know what the impact looks like, while with uncertainty, you don't know what is going to happen next, and you don't even know what the possible impact may look like. That is why risk can be more comprehensively accounted for than uncertainty. Actually you can consider risk as the uncertainty that matters.

Risk are known unknowns. If you're planning to pick up a friend from the airport, the probability that their flight will arrive several hours late is a Risk – you know in advance that the arrival time can change, so you plan accordingly. Uncertainty are unknown unknowns. You may be late picking up your friend from the airport because a meteorite demolishes your car an hour before you planned to leave for the airport. Who could predict that? You can't reliably predict the future based on the past events in the face of Uncertainty. (Josh Kaufman-The Personal MBA) Moreover the "uncertainty" might involve positive or negative unpredictable events of high impact to your life. Therefore to increase your chances of meeting positive events in your life you need to be prepared and position yourself where they proliferate.

A harsh reality, that I personally experienced, is war and political turmoil, which represents a real threat to people's freedom and lives. An example is what happened to many Arab countries starting in 2011, as a series of anti-government protests and uprisings that spread across the whole region. Prior to the ignition of this wave of popular revolutions which was faced in most of the cases by aggressive and brutal reaction from the ruling, regimes of these countries, there was a large amount of uncertainty amongst ordinary people about what was going to happen. On the other side of the scene, the dictators who were ruling with iron fists were ready to deal aggressively with that potential risk to their existence. The economic side of such situations can help in clarifying the relationship between uncertainty and risk, as seemingly endless political turmoil severely impacted the economic situation in these countries. Many industries were suffering, and a lot of multinational companies decided to shut down their operations and leave the regions after suffering severe losses. Only a few managed to keep their operations running profitably, or at least run away at the right time, thereby avoiding significant hits.

The reason behind this is that the companies that managed to survive in such terrible economic situations had to deal with uncertainty as being a major component of risk itself. They had the appetite to manage things that are about to happen, which are easier to estimate than those further out in the future. They knew how to mitigate or even remove things that inhibit effective decision-making or negatively affect performance. They were capable to identify, quantify, and absorb risk whenever possible. Therefore their leadership succeeded to manage the overall situation through a comprehensive risk management approach, rather than gazing into a crystal ball.

Why would you take risk?

When you want to do something in your life or work that feels like a bit of a risk, it can feel appalling and scary. Such feelings can become so self-consuming up to the level that they can stop you from taking the action that could take you away from the risk. But if risk-taking is an act of sacrificing your personal emotions, energy, time, and money, why would you do it?

The answer is because taking risk, also, has a pattern of benefits that comes with it, and that motivates some people to do whatever it takes to captivate these benefits. On the other hand, it seems that the human mind and body craves danger, as risk-taking causes real changes in the human brain. Major risks stimulate your brain to release adrenaline, which can lead to a quick rush, and dopamine, which causes intense feelings of pleasure.

Risk-taking is part of your everyday life, as almost everything you do in life has a percentage of risk in it. Risks needn't be death-defying. Risks can be anything that pushes you past your perceived comfort zone. Do you want to know how I feel when I take a calculated risk in my life? I feel revitalized because taking some risk makes me excited, and that makes me happy. I strongly believe that you should plan to take certain risks in your life. I call these risks the "five magic catalysts for growth and fulfillment" which are:

The risk of failing or mistaking

Embracing risk helps you to overcome the fear of failure, which is, in my opinion, the single biggest obstacle that prevents you from reaching your full potential. Taking risks can result in a positive outcome as you'll never know if you can succeed unless you venture out into new territory. By taking the risk, you are doing yourself a great favor as you drain your tendency for uprightness and doing everything in an ideal way to satisfy the world around you.

In your life or business endeavors, Don't get "analysis paralysis", yet when you feel you've reached a reasonable level of planning and readiness, move on don't hesitate or shrink and don't seek perfection, execute, get the experience, correct yourself and always stay in a continuous mode of action. This is called the power of GEMO (Good Enough Move On). If you don't risk failing, then you can't succeed. Success simply requires risking failure.

The risk of discovering new ways to do things

Are you the kind of person who likes trying new foods every time you go out for dinner, or do you prefer to eat what you already know you like? I always wonder why some people flourish on routine, finding themselves perfectly happy to do the same things day after day. In my opinion, one reason why some people resist trying new things and prefer routine is the fear of the unknown. Studies suggest you fear an unknown outcome more than you do a known bad one. So, to avoid staying frozen from moving forward with new actions or discovering new ways that might make your life happier and more successful, you need to uncover your personal motivation and check if you really want to do these things or not. Ask yourself what specifically you fear to happen if you do this new thing? Courageously face your fears, Cut out closures and stay clear about the probability and impact of any potential risk. Seek help or coaching from someone who knows how to deal with such situations, in case you need that. Just do it and always remember if you face your fear it'll disappear.

The risk of being rejected

The fear of being rejected might be a great challenge for you when you rage against the status quo and take calculated risk to achieve progress in life, it is obvious when you fear, perhaps more than anything else you lose approval from others. In fact, you can't inhibit others from rejecting what you do or what you offer to them, but you can control your worry about being rejected through controlling your emotions, mindset, and reactions.

For example, if you say 'no' occasionally, you're respecting your own needs, which will enhance your self-confidence to a level by which you'll understand and respect others when they say 'no' to you.

It's important to understand that your negative thoughts are a distortion of the truth. The key is to change your negative thoughts and replace them with healthy ones. Realize that everyone gets rejected sometimes. There's no shame in that. Also, understand that it doesn't mean that everyone will reject you just because one person does.

My experience of working as a sales person was the perfect training for me to go into public life because it allowed me to learn how to accept rejection, meet new people and find common ground while working with them. When ten doors are slammed in my face, I go to door number eleven enthusiastically, with a smile on my face. Really, if you don't ask, you won't be answered.

The risk of losing someone or something

When you are faced with new risks, it's easy to shrink back in fear of losing current accouterment or relations rather than see the new opportunities to acquire more benefits and values. Some relationships can be great, but they can also be very restrictive. Following your dreams usually involves quite a bit of isolation. Some partnerships make it very difficult to take the time that you need to get the work done. In my opinion, relationships should support you and your dreams no matter what. You should understand that you may have to distance yourself a bit more and then work interdependently to keep the partnership alive. In life or business, it is more important to go for what is strategically right even if you lose what seems to be immediately profitable. Losing something is not always sad.

The risk of being criticized

Aristotle once said, "Criticism is something you can easily avoid by saying nothing, doing nothing, and being nothing." In life, regardless of who you are or what you are trying to say or do, someone at some point will criticize you. The question here is; is what you stand for strong enough to overcome your fear of being judged and to do it anyway? In fact, the more attention your work receives, the more criticism you'll have to field. As well, you need to be aware that the more time you spend worrying about what someone said, the less time you have to do something about it. In fact, I would be rather grateful to anyone who criticizes me rather than fighting and creating conflicts.

Why don't you choose to think that the people around you want to provide you with help, so you can take this as an opportunity to enhance the relationship with others? In the workplace, as well as anywhere else, next time you receive criticism from anyone, enjoy doing the following:

1. Hold yourself from reacting immediately.
2. Don't take it personally.
3. Listen for understanding.
4. Concentrate on the issue more than the critic.
5. Say thank you.
6. Ask questions to analyze the feedback.
7. Request time to follow up.
8. Take it as a chance to improve.

Domesticating the risk

Managing risk is not recklessness; it is an ability to convert the dangerous event into a domesticated condition, and sometimes a useful one. You can't do this without having the right mindset, and being able to pursue effective decision making.

So what is risk management? It is the process of identifying risk, assessing risk, and taking steps to reduce risk to an acceptable level. By doing this frequently in life, you become more confident and risk tolerable. The consequence of exposure to a sub-lethal level of the risk may result in the development of resistance to higher levels; this is known as acclimation to risk, which is something you do in your daily life. A good example of this occurs when learning to drive a car. At first, a new driver may fear traveling on freeways, but over time that same driver with more experience will merge casually into speeding traffic with little consideration for the significant potential dangers.

In case you are starting a new project in your life, whether it is a start-up business or renovating your house or developing a new software application or any similar endeavor, a risk management plan should be a part of your overall project plan. The risk plan for smaller projects can be as simple as a risk management matrix, while complex projects require more thorough risk analysis and planning. When you have such tool in hand, you'll be able to eliminate most of the potentially related risks to your business.

The methodology to create your risk management matrix usually goes through the following steps:

Brainstorm risks before you begin your project. Scan ahead by reaching out into the future for ideas, information, or instincts. Listen constantly for "faint signals" of what may become significant. Make linkages between different signals to form patterns.

Identify and list what risks can be associated with the project. Will the risks affect the schedule, resourcing or budget?

Estimate the probability of each potential risk occurring. Put a percentage or a number for each one.

Think about the impact of each risk on your project if it really were to occur. Use a scale appropriate for your project, perhaps from 1-5.

Now you can determine the priority of each risk by simply multiplying the probability by impact. Higher priority items should be mitigated and planned for before lower priority items.

Move on and establish a mitigation response, which is in nature a brief overview of mitigation steps to eliminate or reduce the risk. What exactly are the actions you need to do to stay free of a risk impact? You also need to know who will support you in dealing with this risk. And when is the exact time to interfere?

The above mentioned steps are a generic methodology to plan and manage risks in projects, which you can also use in many other life domains, such as your health, career, and financial life.

Meanwhile, for your health thriving, a set of preventive measures to mitigate health-related risks could be done by constantly working to keep your mind, soul, and body as much as you can away from serious risks. Therefore try to:

Exercise regularly, a minimum of four times per week for 30 minutes or more.

Eat plenty of fresh fruit and vegetables. Eat good fats such as those found in salmon, tuna, mackerel, avocados, nuts, and take Omega 3 fish oil daily.

Reduce your alcohol intake and target to quit it completely. Don't turn to it in times of stress -- instead, drink water and go for a walk. Never smoke as this is not good for your health either.

Allow yourself quiet time to relax, learn deep breathing techniques to help manage any anxiety, talk about your problems with someone you can trust and if necessary seek professional help.

Likewise, career risks need a mitigation plan to decrease the likelihood of career problems, such as being laid off, fired, or having difficulty in finding a job. The following tips should help you minimizing your career risk:

Optimize your network with others within your industry. Networking will help you if something happens to your current job. Also, it makes you more exposed to many experiences and talents. For this reason, also keep your resume up to date, so you are ready for anything.

Try always to think about how you can best help the company you work for to be more successful and continue to grow

Have the uncompromised commitment to your organization ethics and compliance, and never break laws. Always look after your personal and professional reputation.

By the same token, your financial security and wellbeing are very much related to your ability to manage any potential risk to your income. For example, the following strategies can help you leverage your financial stability:

Diversify your income sources by investing early to allow your money to start working for you. Think of your money as yet another income generator for your household.

Max out your retirement savings. It goes without saying that how much you contribute to your retirement account will make a big difference over time.

Do your best to have the optimum insurance coverage for health, car, properties and other important things in your life, and make sure to keep policies up to date and sufficient for your circumstances.

Build an emergency fund to cover yourself for a reasonable period in case any unfavorable events happen. You should have a high yield savings account or any similar funds.

Pay in cash and receive in cash for everything you can, and use your credit cards only in emergencies. Try always to avoid interest fees, finance charges, and late payment fees, and don't get trapped into the habit of buying what you can't afford.

Give generously and make a regular contribution to charity and community.

Always have a "will", as well as health and financial powers of attorney in case of a disaster.

A final word in this chapter is that risk-taking in life and business should be like salt in food; a little can enhance the flavor, but too much can spoil the pleasure. Risk has its disadvantages; that is why it is called risk, so don't be addicted to it, but learn how to pick the deserving adventure to hunt your precious target. Always diversify your life alternatives and stay sharply focused on what does matter and lies within your span of control.

CHAPTER 8

BE RESILIENT

"Inside of a ring or out, ain't nothing wrong with going down. It's staying down that's wrong." That is the way the legendary *Mohamed Ali* put it. And that was, in my opinion, his leadership secret.

There are many incidences in Mohamed Ali's life that show an inspiring resilience and extraordinary persistence, such as what happened to him in 1967 when the United States was at war in Vietnam, Ali refused to be inducted into the armed forces, saying "I ain't got a quarrel with those Vietcong." On June 20, 1967, Ali was convicted of draft evasion, sentenced to five years in prison, fined $10,000 and banned from boxing for three years. He stayed out of prison as his case was appealed, and he was returned to the ring on October 26, 1970. When he returned to the boxing ring to reclaim his title, fascinating the public with marathon fights against *Joe Frazier* and *George Foreman*, Ali became almost the most famous person in the world at that time. Around 30 years after, Mohamed Ali, suffering from Parkinson's Disease, surprised the whole world by lighting the flame in the opening ceremonies of the Olympic games in Atlanta in 1996. At that moment, I remembered his inspiring quote, "I hated every minute of training, but I said, 'Don't quit.

Suffer now and live the rest of your life as a champion"

Resilience is accepting your new reality, even if it's not as good as the one you had before. It is your ability to stand strong and calm, and do what you should do in the face of stressors and challenges. Instead of whining, stand up again and work to win. It is an amazing enabler in managing uncertainty; with it, your reaction to life changes will be positive and constructive.

My wife and I love the movie "The Pursuit of Happiness," that was based on the real story of entrepreneur *Chris Gardner*. The film features *Will Smith* as Gardner, who is presented as a homeless salesman. Smith's son *Jaden Smith* co-stars, making his film debut as *Gardner's* son, *Christopher Jr.* It is really one of our favorite movies ever, because it is full of life's lessons, especially how to be persistent and resilient in the face of a tough and uncertain life. In the movie, Chris loses his house, goes to a motel, and eventually he ends up living in a homeless shelter. He and his son even spend a night in a subway station restroom. Life humiliates him. He tastes bitterness and then tastes happiness. So if your story in life begins with ghastly things happening to you, this doesn't mean things will always end badly. With resilience, you manage to overcome hardships and misfortune and navigate your way to better opportunities in life.

As a creature of God, who enables you with the needed power to face what you should face, stay assured that you are looked after, and everything always works out for you. So never belittle yourself, and never give up.

As a leader, you may feel uncertain, but you must be able to show that you are strong and that you know what you're doing to yourself as well as to others. Sometimes you take one or two steps back, aiming to rebound and reach a higher level. This is how resilience serves ambition. Always remember: "The oak fought the wind and was broken, the willow bent when it must and survived." (*Robert Jordan*)

The surprising resilience

During the last five years of my life, I had the chance to be very close to the sorrows of many people who had to leave their homeland due to wars or significant threats to their rights as humans. I lived close to many of them in different places around the world. I was able to create friendship with some of them. In fact, I learned a lot from their agonizing life experience; I heard many painful stories about their lives, which had been dramatically changed due to the war on their homeland. Despite of being traumatized, most refugees I got to know were surprisingly resilient.

When I used to visit my Syrian friend who was running a restaurant nearby my house in Cairo and had our sweet chat over a cup of tea, I wondered how he could in very short time stand again on his feet after escaping the lethal war and the brutality of the ruling regime back home. I'm always surprised by the resilience of these people, the way they can continue and thrive in the context of difficulty. After either surviving a deadly sea on a rubber boat or crossing the borders from country to country carrying their children and facing the harsh weather and greedy smugglers, the ones who manage to arrive at a new destination feel as if they have been given a new life.

During my stay in *Istanbul-Turkey* in the last three years, I knew many refugees, who despite their tough living situations were also involved in volunteering activities such as education, health care or other programs to support the rest of their suffering communities. Their daily marathons to provide the basic life needs for themselves and their families didn't hide their high sense of dignity and willingness to pursue happiness.

A well-known story about two Syrian swimmers, *Sarah and Yusra Mardini*, describes well the essence of resilience. As In August 2015, Sarah and her younger sister Yusra took the hazardous route to *Lesvos* Island in Greece by themselves, as refugees fleeing the war in their motherland Syria. The women, who are trained elite swimmers, captivated audiences around the world, first because of their rescue of their 18 fellow passengers after their boat's engine failed, and again when 18-year-old Yusra made history as she competed in Rio Olympics as part of the first-ever Refugee Olympic Team. Sarah returned to Lesvos as a volunteer lifeguard with Emergency Response Centre International (ERCI), a Greek non-profit humanitarian organization that assists refugees in distress as they attempt to reach the island. She took them through it as she has also been through it once before and she know how does it really feel!

Truly, trauma causes you to discover your genuine motivation and purpose in life, and resilience helps you to navigate and negotiate successfully for your wellbeing.

Cancel and continue

Have you ever seen a baby who learns to walk, a child who learns to ride a bike, or an adult who learn how to drive a car?

They all look the same, as they stagger and fall numerous times before getting it right. It takes failure after failure to create success.

Mistakes are learning opportunities. So you need to have sufficient courage to make mistakes. And never regret anything, because every little detail of your life, including your mistakes, is what made you who you are today. If you just accept making them, mistakes can improve your self-awareness, and teach you how to think and do in a better way. Mistakes are there to make you humble, and better at accepting yourself and others.

In gymnastics; even the most elite gymnasts make mistakes. But they learn how not to allow these mistakes to bother them as this can mess up their performance and overall self-confidence. In gymnastics, professional coaches never, ever rebuke a gymnast for making a mistake in their routine at a competition, or on any other occasion. If a gymnast makes a mistake in a competition, they know. They don't need to be reminded or told. The important thing is how they recover from these mistakes and tackle the rest of the competition. This is what will ultimately shape them as a great competitive athlete.

Life didn't come with a user manual, so accept that mistakes will happen to you. You are not your mistakes, you are not your shortage, and you are here at this moment with the power to shape your present and your future. No matter how chaotic the past has been, the future is a clean and fresh opportunity. What you do with it is up to you. When you make a mistake, it's important that you don't fall into the trap of trying to justify your mistake. Mistakes must be contained, not justified. Unless you take responsibility for your mistakes, you will never learn how to move forward in your life.

I personally know one of today's prominent consultants in the field of hospital sterilization and infection prevention. He teaches medical staff all over the world. This person once told me a sad story which happened to him at the very beginning of his career life, as he was at that time an operation room nurse, working in one of the hospitals in his city. That day he was serving in an ear operation where the patient was supposed to make an ear graft. By mistake, he mixed up the trays, which he had to take away into the garbage. The one that he threw away in the unsterile bin was the one that included the patient autograft. After almost 40 years from the time of this incident, he still remembers what happened. He was named, blamed and shamed. The story was even published in one of the local newspapers. It was a great lesson for him, which he benefited from for the rest of his life. According to him, no one is immune from making mistakes, and when they occur, they give you an opportunity to grow stronger. This story and other similar stories makes me aware that even in the best of worlds people do make mistakes, and these are not to be denied or hidden, but worked around.

One dark cloud can't cover the entire sky. The sun is always shining on some parts of your life. Pay the cost of your setback but never break down; think of what you deserve, and keep pushing forward. It is not the end of the world.

Lead with Resilience

Real leaders deal with resilience as a strategic approach to embracing change that addresses both downside and upside possibilities. In business planning, resilience means that everybody knows exactly what the goal they are trying to achieve is, but also that the path to it is not carved into stone. Each project has so many variables that cannot be foreseen; projects can take longer than expected, customer feedback can turn everything upside-down, even the project fundamental assumptions can change during the execution. I'm sure you've seen it happen.

Actually, strategic planning improves the leader's ability to foresee problems and allocate resources appropriately but, rigid strategic planning can sometimes be too firm, and not allowing for the changing demands. However, having no plan can result in a lack of direction. That is why having a versatile plan often allows for alternative scenarios and solutions that can be used if needed. I believe that a good plan should deal with:

- Operational resilience, which is the ability to quickly adjust your offers.
- Financial resilience, which is the ability to quickly access and deploy financial resources.
- Organizational resilience, which is the ability to quickly adapt the organization's structure to address external and internal pressures and achieve targets.
- Technological resilience, which is the ability to quickly change technological capability to meet market needs.

Organizations might face tough times, like a drop in revenues or market uncertainty. They all need to believe that things will be ok, that tomorrow or next week or next year will be better. It is vital for you as a leader to be flexible in your way of managing complex situations, especially with the uncertainty surrounding many things in today's life. Your ability to modify your usual ways of problem-solving and adapt to more practical ways can be life-saving to your organization. You should acknowledge others' ideas and concerns; you need to validate assumptions in multiple ways, such as consulting, discussing, and reviewing. Take your time to explore the problematic areas with people who might be affected by them, and help them to understand the need for flexibility and change to survive. Stand up for difficulties that a change may imply, and negotiate openly to find a course of action that copes with the difficulties perceived by key stakeholders in your business.

Openness to learning and change is a crucial personality trait for you as a leader who must adapt to changing conditions. In the same way, your emotional intelligence should drive you to empathize with others' feelings, which is essential for determining how to influence and motivate them.

Building resilience

One of the most inspiring sports moments happened last year during the Rio Olympics, as millions over the world watched the 33-year-old British track and field athlete, Mo Farah, overcame a mid-race fall and drive out of the field in the final 100m of the 10,000-meter race, to win in 27 minutes and five seconds.

The most successful British track athlete in modern Olympic Games history, Mo described how he felt in that critical moment by saying, "When I felt I was just thinking 'try and get back as fast as you can,' I was thinking 'don't panic, don't panic, and don't panic.' At one moment, I thought my dream was over, my race was over. I tried to be tough, and that is what I did."

This story and other similar ones often make me think, why do some people bounce back from adversity and hardships while others break down? The key word behind this, in my opinion, is resilience. Resilience involves behaviors, thoughts, and actions that can be learned and developed in anyone.

No one's life is less off stressors and hardships, but some people are better at maintaining flexibility and balance in their life when they deal with stressful circumstances and traumatic events. Those people are actually more enabled to deal with uncertainty in life and to reach a higher level of achievement and self-actualization.

So whether it is dealing with unemployment, a difficult relationship or any personal misfortunes, you need to learn how to overcome irrational fears of change and boost your self-confidence. The following five tips will help you in establishing the right mindset and building the needed resilience in dealing with life challenges:

Accept change as part of your life

Certain long-term goals may no longer be possible as a result of adverse situations. Accepting conditions that cannot be changed can help you focus on conditions that you can alter. As an adult, you can't be taller, but for sure you can do something better regarding your weight if you need to.

Foster a positive view of yourself

Focus on your strength, build on your success and always surround yourself with positive people. Developing confidence in your ability to solve problems and trusting your instincts always help build your resilience. Positive opportunities will naturally transform your mind and give you the ability to effortlessly manifest success factors in every area of your life.

Stretch yourself

As in sport, fitness is not only fast or strong, but it is also stretch ability and flexibility. The more you stretch yourself by accepting new challenges that require new skills, the more resilient you'll become in life.

Pursue opportunities for self-discovery

Use different opportunities to discover the way you think and perform, and in so doing maximize your self-awareness and replace negative attitudes with positive ones. Generally speaking, people who are self-aware are more likely to show flexibility in life and in business.

Take care of yourself

Physical, spiritual, and emotional health is all connected; that is why you need to pay attention to your personal needs. Engage yourself from time to time in activities that you enjoy and find relaxing and motivating. Exercise regularly, have a good body shape, and a fresh mind. Taking care of "you" helps to keep your soul, mind, and body prepared to deal with situations that require resilience.

God created you to be a highly capable and creative problem-solver who can become stronger and more flexible in stressful times. So, with ups and downs in life, it is important not to regret what you've been through. Always push yourself to deal with different life incidents in a simple and balanced way, so that you don't have to be sad over things that you fail to get, or over-rejoice because of which you succeeded to win.

CHAPTER 9

BE SIMPLE

Have you ever wondered why so many people still love black and white photos? There are many reasons for feeling attracted and inspired by the beauty of such photos; for me, it is the brilliant sense of simplicity which is embedded in them. Black and white photographs push away the distraction coming from different colors, and emphasize the relationship between subject and background. It makes my brain more relaxed and my soul more nourished.

In today's life, the fine demarcation between black and white, right and wrong is not so visible. The rules have been blurred, and the uncertainty about the future is like never before. I sometimes feel that I need a filter to take away the distraction and haziness that invade my mind and soul every day in life. I believe that the following three behaviors that are widely represented in our today's life, strongly contribute to making our life less simple and more uncertain.

Consumerism

This is seen in our everyday consumption of goods and materials, and in the way, some people run everywhere after brands and image-satisfying products or services. Consumerism becomes a dominant socio-economic order and ideology; as today's vast productive economy demands that you make consumption your way of life. But would this make you happy and secure? Even if some "consumption addicts" can swim through life with little distress, consumerism carries larger costs that are worth worrying about. These costs make your certainty of economy, health, environment, and relationship ever decreasing. The problem is that, when you begin consuming more than what you need, boundaries get removed.

Material things are neither bad nor good; what is important is what they bring to your life that makes it truly and simply happy and meaningful. Thus, you need to think of the important life components, which you can't buy from a mall or a supermarket; the intangible things like love, trust, and faith.

Competition

Overwhelming competition is another reason for making our today's life less happy and more apprehensive. I grew up believing that competition "brings out the best" in people. But is this true? When I think of jealousy, distrust, bitterness and protectiveness, I always see them as creatures of competition. Competition usually makes you focus on others' lives rather than your own. Of course, one side of human nature is self-interest, to do whatever you can to survive and thrive, often at the expense of others. But the real problem appears with not controlling and overdoing this behavior, because it destroys your sense of peacefulness and turns you into a selfish and aggressive individual.

Have you ever thought, why do some governments decide to throw extra agriculture products into the ocean while millions of people In Africa are living deadly famines? Or why do some companies over-market certain drugs and enhance over-prescription of them, even at the expense of children's health and families' economy? It is the evil competition.

Ironically, many researches stated that in workplaces people who help others without seeking anything in return are more successful in the long term than people who try to maximize benefits only for themselves.

For society as a whole, the *World Happiness Report 2013*, a major global study, found that two of the strongest explanatory factors for national wellbeing are levels of social support and generosity. Success as a society directly depends on the extent to which you see others as a source of support rather than as a source of threat.

Perfectionism

Seeking simplicity in all that you do helps you set easier expectations and goals for yourself, which consequently reduces your uncertainty about life. But some people who are known as perfectionists strive for flawlessness in everything they do in life. They always tend to complicate things and set exceedingly high performance standards for themselves. They are known to be extremely critical when evaluating their own efforts and results.

You need to know that there is no way to have a simple life if everything has to be perfect, as the perfect pie takes a lot longer to make than the good enough one. The simple life is a life that makes you live happily without feeling distressed. But, perfectionism might steal that simple life when you push yourself to have a perfect job, partner, house, kids, car, etc.

Think simply

You and I live in an age of terrifying complexity. There's more information, applications, communication, and options to choose from than ever before. Thousands of complex operating systems are everywhere surrounding you. In many cases, your brain seems to be the noisiest place on the earth, even if you are alone and distant from others.

Do you overthink every little problem until it becomes bigger than it is? Do you overthink positive things until they don't look so positive anymore? If you are, I believe you need to rethink your way of thinking.

It is very easy to get paralyzed by overthinking problems in life or business, and this might make you less confident in your ability to solve these problems, so you become more and more uncertain about what you are doing. To avoid getting trapped in this vicious circle, you need to learn how to think in a simpler way, maybe like a six-year-old child. You can't believe how amazing it is taking a child's point of view. It is in my opinion the best way to tackle a problem or to create something new as it will give you a fresh perspective on everything you do, you'll find much fewer limitations to what you think about, you'll have more fun with the thinking process itself, you'll be fearless of other's judgment on you, and the most important thing is that you'll feel that amazing desire to question everything to satisfy your curiosity.

Have you noticed that the most effective people are almost truly simple? Have you noticed that in life and business, smarter solutions always come from a simpler way of thinking? You can make faster and better decisions when you are simple because you only need to think of a few factors; you don't need to dig deep in an abundance of data and analysis as you are trying to predict the future by analyzing the past, which is by nature a poor predictor of the future.

I love to collect simple information about business or life cases through casual chatting, rather than formal interviewing. And I always seek an outsider's opinion, whether this outsider is an expert, friend, or sometimes my ten-year-old son.

I never use more than three basic guiding rules to decide on something. I create these rules after revisiting my purpose, and knowing what the bottlenecks and available alternatives are. This habit makes my life easy and productive as I can always remember these few basic rules and stick to them. I rethink my rules only if they are no longer working, if the overall situation has changed, or if I discover better ways to do things. If you have too firm guidelines in your life, you should be worried, as they are the definitive product of lazy thinking.

Another effective, simple yet rarely used technique to improve one's way of thinking and make it simpler is meditation. You can practice it; simply by relaxing your mind and nourishing your soul with healthy thoughts and spiritual reflections, you'll enjoy the amazing mind clarity and feel the positive energy within yourself.

Lead simply

Leadership doesn't have to be complex. In fact, leadership can be very easy. If you are leading people, it is in your hand to make it easy for everyone to accomplish his or her personal objectives while ensuring that the whole team is pursuing their collective mission.

In my opinion, simple leadership is all about simple communication, as nothing ignites execution like clear objectives, simple strategies, and motivating reward. That is specifically what you have to create, and effectively communicate as a leader.

Avoid excess jargon and complex messages when communicating with your people, and work to clean the whole organization from its negative confusing effect. Instead, use words that clearly describe the business' mission, vision, and strategies. Go back to the basics, so the mission is what your assignment is, the vision is where do you want to be in the longer term, and the strategy is how can you reach there? When you execute always be practical; plan simply then implement, evaluate, and correct yourself if needed and continue acting in a better way. When you feel that your vision, mission, goals and strategy are clearly communicated, and you get your team to buy into it, this is your right time to stop micromanaging. So step back and let the team innovate. You supposedly have selected good people to do the job so let them do it. Go monitor the gauges and enjoy leading the ship.

As a leader it is your duty to facilitate work discussions and meetings so that people build agreements, make quality decisions and create realistic action plans. Always involve people in decision-making to improve the quality of decisions and increase commitment to implementation. It is your role to simplify your organizational structure to the optimum level, which allows doing its core function smoothly. Always coach others in a way that facilitates clear thinking, personal responsibility, and creative problem-solving, and never forget to celebrate success whenever it happens, even in a simple way.

One of the qualities of smart leaders is that they are aware of how much they don't know; that is why they are the best leaders. They haven't claimed they know it all, but they have the unyielding desire to learn from others. Successful leaders also admit to making mistakes. They are simply transparent to themselves and others who may benefit from their experience. Only simple leaders have this wisdom while many others lack it.

Live Simply

In today's hectic life, when you hear about simplifying life, you may think it means moving into a relaxing home on an isolated island and living off the land, spending your days by the beach and enjoying nature. But that is not necessarily a simpler life, and it may not be for everyone. In my opinion, simply living is a decision to find joy and peace within the simple things in your life. Thus you need to take care not just of the visible things in your everyday life, such as your physical space, nutrition, attire, but you also need to manage what is going on in your spiritual life. Here are some important approaches for a simple life that you need to understand and practice consistently.

Design a life that's simply fitting for you.

Your life is your life. It should make sense to you. You should live it a way that makes you live your core values in everything you do, so you can be yourself and not what others expect you to be. Take time to consider what makes up the spirit of who you are. Try to think about what kinds of things you would or wouldn't like to do, and act accordingly; finding out through trial and error helps more than you may think it does. And always remember, just because society says so about something, doesn't mean it is so.

Live within today

Don't waste your life recalling the past or worrying about the future. You can't change or control either one. So save your time and energy for today. You can enjoy today and get the maximum value of it, but you can't do this for the past or the future. It is always the "journey" that will determine your destination, so do your best in the moment. Work seriously, love gratefully, give generously, and don't fixate on future or past events that would make you miss the essence of today.

Live within your means

Living within your means is more than just balancing your budget. You basically need to be aware of the difference between what is essential and what is nice to have. You need to adapt yourself to spend what is less than the amount of money you bring in each month. The uncertain future and the turbulent economy are always calling you to develop lifelong habits of frugality, and avoid wasteful consumption. Learn how to find happiness in life with the things available to you, more than the ones that are not available yet.

Don't rush

When you rush, you miss many of your life's beauties, and you expose yourself to much suffering. Life is not a race. There is no competition, so enjoy everything you do by doing it meaningfully and slowly. Talk slowly, drive slowly and eat slowly. Don't rush your quality time. Don't rush establishing or ending a relationship, don't rush to be critical of someone or something. Take your time to make commitments in life and never rush on your communication, especially when you have to express your feelings. Be punctual and never miss a deadline, simply by taking the enough needed time to deliver what you have to deliver.

Relax

Like everyone else, you will sometimes feel frazzled and overwhelmed due to life stressors. You don't need to book a flight to a Caribbean island to spend a week on the beach to relax yourself each time you feel stressed. There are many simple ways in life to make you feel tranquil and to restore your peace of mind and energy, such as worship, meditation, deep breathing techniques, visualizing being in a place that relaxes you. Make healthy dietary choices and drink fresh water, and so forth. Another good and simple way to keep you relaxed is to always be prepared, as the more prepared you are for a certain stress-inducing activity, the less stressed you will feel.

Reduce your commitments

From now forward take on fewer commitments. Drop those that aren't in line with your life priorities. When you deal with an obligation, know exactly what needs to get done as the stress of an obligation is sometimes greater than the obligation itself. Identify exactly what action items you need to take, and maybe your stress levels will reduce. You may struggle at first, but focus your intent on simplifying your life, which will bring about peace.

Clear up your schedule

Make a list of all of the things that are on your mind at this moment: plans, projects, tasks, and commitments. Find ways to free up your time for the important stuff. That means eliminating the stuff you don't like, cutting back on time wasters, and making room for what you want to do. Go through your list and identify the things that are weighing most heavily on your mind. Decide which obligations, if any, you can let go of to ease the stress and make your day more simple and fun.

Have more engaged relationships

Nowadays it's truly hard to connect with anyone when you are hyper-connected to your computers and phones. Unplugging gives you tranquility and allows you time for engagement. Spend time with people you love; surround yourself with simple and faithful people. If you are lucky to have two parents, or one of them is still alive, stay close to them, take care of them; treat them with compassion and mercy as they took care of you when you were young.

Declutter your life

Excessive clutter can make you more stressed; it is a major contributor to uncertainty in life as it continuously feeds your subconscious with that sense of vulnerability and worry. Decluttering your home, workplace in addition to your digital space can lead to a less cluttered mind. The simplest way to succeed in this mission is to take things one small step at a time. For you to have a more organized simple life always start from priorities, establish a simple morning and evening routine and stick to it. Have some help regarding physical decluttering if you need as this will help you to avoid chaotic days and will elevate your morale.

CHAPTER 10

BE PART OF THE EXPERIENCE

"By three methods we may learn wisdom:
First, by reflection, which is noblest;
second, by imitation, which is easiest; and third
by experience, which is the bitterest."
— Confucius

When everything is changing fast around you, or when you feel uncertain about many things in life, it seems that there is no other way to understand what is going on or to predict future consequence than to induce a new life experiment and be part of it; so you can break this vicious circle and move forward. I believe that it is the right way to challenge your emotional states, biases and fears. Your struggle to pursue certainty in life is not like a game to win or lose, but it is more about fully living the experience itself. It is the choices that you make, depending not just on economic implications, but also on the nature and extent of scrutiny by others.

Seeking happiness, wisdom or security in life is not a shopping experience; it is a full spiritual experience that you have to embrace by yourself. For example, if you are stuck in your career and see no gain or development happening to you through it, but rather more deviation from your original goals, in such case you might be open to a new experience aiming to explore a new way of doing things better, at the same time to reduce your uncertainty. Maybe you will decide to quit your job and start up your own business. Or maybe you want to leave the whole industry and figure out a more suitable one. Whatever you are looking for, you need to know that it involves knowledge, risk, difficulties, and for sure some pain.

Even though what you intend to do is not a lab experience but a real life one, you need to start from the lab side. Where you work to create a design for the whole thing, starting by analyzing the gap between where you are right now and where you want to be, then set a plan of action and, most important, monitoring and evaluation methods through which you can measure your progress. Like any experiment, you need also to provide the needed tools, materials and budget.

Did curiosity really kill the cat?

Cats have natural instinct to investigate, discover, and explore. It seems that this instinct fosters their intelligence, and maybe that is why many people love them. In my opinion, it is not always the case that curiosity is a cat killer, but it is always the fulfillment that came because of its unstoppable curiosity that makes it happy and vital. Your strong desire to know or learn something strange or unusual is your key to winning your game against uncertainty, while apathy or indifference is more likely to increase your vulnerability. When you leave your comfort zone to embrace a new life experience, you will test what you read before in books about wisdom and patience. Your curiosity will take you on a venture that you might not enjoy right then and there, but when you look back at what you've done, you'll feel like ... "yeah."

Don't expect any excitement or freedom in your comfort zone. Jail might be the safest place in the whole world but, as you know, there is no freedom there. If you really want to grow up, the first thing you need to do is to jump outside your comfort zone and then experiment and be part of the new experience. While pursuing this be aware that you're allowed to be less than perfect; God loves imperfect people as we all make mistakes. The worst thing that can happen when you try something new is that you might fail but can you imagine how much could you learn from this failure so you can be successful next time? At least you'll not follow the same wrong way again, and you probably learned that it wasn't as scary as you imagined. The beautiful thing about getting out of your comfort zone is that you'll increase your tolerance for risk taking, and enjoy that thrilling sensation of freedom and involvement.

Experimenting might make you feel strange but it is ok to look strange or extraordinary. You may find that people like you more for being so. Expect more doors to be open in your face as you're a real unusual exploring savvy. Do something you normally wouldn't do for fear of looking abnormal. Be that abnormal. You'll be fine.

I recently read in a newspaper that a 70-year-old woman once told a stunt pilot named *Aragon* that she'd love to learn to fly, but thought she was too old. *Aragon* replied: "There's an 85-year-old aerobatic pilot having a great time of it, and she learned when she was older than you." That sounds so consistent with what *Monash University* aged care expert Professor *Joseph Ibrahim* says. As he believes that elderly people should have the right to do what they like in their senior years. Accordingly the Melbourne professor Ibrahim is pushing a new approach to aged care, hoping to spark a discussion about how simple yet risky activities can enrich the lives of those in their senior years.

Entrepreneurship, the thrilling experience

History is telling us that, at the experimentation level, the story of the light bulb begins long before Thomas Edison. If so, why is Thomas Edison usually credited with the invention of this revolutionary technology? The answer, in my opinion, is because he patented the first commercially successful bulb in 1879 before anyone else could. In addition to being a legendary science genius, he was also a great business savvy who patented more than 1000 US patents under his name, and founded the leading company *General Electric*.

Traditionally, an entrepreneur has been defined as a person who starts, organizes, and manages any enterprise, especially a business, usually with considerable initiative and risk, rather than working as an employee. The entrepreneur is commonly seen as a business leader and innovator of new ideas and business processes.

There are many motivations for people to become entrepreneurs. My friend, who resigned his "salary job" and established his technology enterprise, told me that he became an entrepreneur because the idea of working for someone else never sat well with him. That may also make sense to you, in case you have always wanted to oversee your own destiny. Some others who became entrepreneurs were mainly driven by their dreams of becoming wealthy. That is all real. I could say, based on my personal experience in entrepreneurship, that you may embrace a new business venture when you deeply feel that the certainty which is related to your current career path is less important than the uncertainty about a potential future business venture.

When you decide to be an entrepreneur, in fact, you decide to experiment. So you either compete with existing products or services or take a new venture and totally invent a new thing. In both cases, you are fighting against uncertainty, but the real experience says that the second kind of venture is accompanied with a larger amount of uncertainty, as the probabilities and potential outcomes are not known. In both cases, entrepreneurs can optimize their strategy by selecting sectors that are capital-efficient for both experimentation and subsequent scaling, and that generate large returns for successful investments in a short period.

You don't need to be *Sir Richard Branson* or *Bill Gates* to experience entrepreneurship, as many other people do entrepreneur in other ways. For example, an aspiring artist who creates things and then shares them with someone can make a real scalable business out of his creative ventures, especially when he learns how to use marketing and public relations to position himself in the marketplace.

You may have heard the story of the "*Beatles*," who were already well-off in 1964 when *Paul McCartney* and *John Lennon* sat down one day to make a new song. At the time, *Paul* says, "*John* would be getting an extension on his house or something, and the joke used to be, 'Okay! Today let's write a swimming pool.' It was great motivation." *Paul* continues, "Then in the next three hours, 'Help!' appears from nowhere, you'd suddenly get the idea, that'll be a hit, this is a good one. You become aware what you were doing was making good money."

Uncertainty about work experience

I know many people, with 10 or more years of working experience in certain industries, who couldn't find a job when they changed their countries or companies. In some cases, they accepted jobs that were technically two or three levels below their original ones. So let's agree that your many years working "history" may not be enough proof that you are expert in what you are doing.

With experience in leading different teams on a variety of projects and assignments, I found out that work experience is the outcome of multiplying your personal capabilities by the level of your exposure to specific job responsibilities.

Experience = Personal Capabilities × Level of Exposure

"Capabilities" expresses your personal ability to achieve objectives, especially about the overall job mission. Some capabilities, such as intelligence or physical traits, may be inherited, while others are learnable skills such as computing, programming, negotiation, etc. The other variable in this equation is your level of exposure to different work responsibilities in relation to the broad job description and career objective.

So the experience you gain while working in a specific field or occupation is proportionately related to any qualitative or quantitative change in your personal capabilities and/or that of your job assignment (work exposure). It is also correct to assume that negative or positive change in your level of experience may result from self-imposed causes or due to the system itself.

To better explain the above mentioned concept; let us assume that we have two sales persons working in the same field. The first one has only two years working history but he is truly smart, self-esteemed, knowledgeable, resilient, can sell sophisticated solutions, be responsible for covering a large area of the market, and he is always committed to stretched targets. The other sales person carries ten years working history, but has lesser capabilities and work exposure. In that case the first sales person, according to my definition, is more expert in sales than the second one; despite the fact that he is newer to the business. So, when I select people to work with me, I first make sure that they have "values" close to the organizational values. After this, I exhaust myself in selecting the most experienced caliber in relation to the formula mentioned above. You really shouldn't pay much attention to how much years of "work history" candidates put on their resumé, as you have the right tools to measure their personal capabilities and their level of exposure to the needed job specialties.

Advocacy, the life changing experience

Many people around the globe face different types of diversities which increase their vulnerability. The brunt of political, environmental and socio-economic changes, in many cases, results in a wide exposure for weak individuals or groups who become victims to its associated risks.

Carol and her husband John are very active in advocating for child mental health, and their rights for suitable accommodation and assistance at schools. They have a lovely eight-year-old girl who suffers some neurological and mental disorders, which delay her abilities in development through the normal educational system. Attention deficit hyperactivity disorder (ADHD) is one of them. They believe that their child is always their child, regardless of age, and they live with hope to improve the quality of life for her, and for many other kids in the same conditions. They know exactly how does it look and feel, that is why they are also working with other groups to improve the lives of similar children's families.

Over many years in this mission, they accumulated a considerable amount of experience and networking, which allowed them to help many kids and families. One interesting thing about this journey, John said, is that when they were digging deep trying to understand the issues of ADHD in order to be good in advocacy, he discovered that he, himself, has adult (ADD) attention deficit disorder. His doctor told him that many of his academic and career sufferings were due to this disorder. John wonders whether, if he had been aware of this, he might have thought or acted differently about his studies and career.

By supporting and enabling people to express their views and concerns, access information and services, defend and promote their rights and responsibilities, you are living a very valuable life experience. Acting on behalf of others will teach you how to stand up for yourself, voice opinions and make decisions for which you will be accountable. When you support others to explore their choices and options, you are at the same time exploring yourself and strengthening your aptitudes in the face of life uncertainty.

Ethical concerns with experimentation

The kinds of decisions you make during uncertain conditions usually have a set of consequences that you cannot predict. It is, therefore, essential that, whenever you make decisions with unpredictable outcomes, you weigh the possible results. Of course, some decisions carry more severe risks than others, but in cases where your decision affects others' wellbeing and puts their benefits at stake, resolving uncertainty for a better decision becomes an ethical mandate.

Think about what is going on in today's clinical and pharmaceutical trials, where uncertainty is becoming an inherent aspect of clinical practice related to many diseases. Therefore many believe that clinical testing should not be offered with the explicit aim to reduce uncertainty. Rather, uncertainty should be appraised, adapted to and communicated about as a part of the process of offering and providing such information.

As a father, a mother or any leader who is responsible for a wider range of affiliates, you often face a knowledge gap and shortage of time which tends to complicate your decision-making process, especially with uncertainty. In such cases, you need to be precautious and seek an outsider opinion or expert advice to make a decision in light of uncertainties.

ABOUT THE AUTHOR

Mohamed Elshahawy is best described as an expert in developing leadership and achieving growth through talent management and organizational development.

Mohamed was working as a country business leader in the multinational conglomerate 3M before he decided to become an entrepreneur and resume his career as a corporate trainer and business consultant who helped many organizations and individuals to develop their business in many areas around the world.

He is an energetic professional speaker with a big heart and diversified life experience, which always guarantees his audiences that they will walk away from his events with tools to execute immediately in their life and business.

Born in Egypt and living now in Canada, he has both a medical degree and a masters in international business administration.

During the 2012 presidential election in Egypt, Mohamed was the campaign general manager of the presidential candidate Dr. Abdulmonem Aboelfotouh.

Mohamed's social and business network, which exists in different areas in the world, has allowed him to be a cross-cultural differences expert, and always give him a real faith in human power.

You can contact Mohamed via email at mmshahawy@yahoo.com. He would love to hear about your experience in regard to what you have implemented from this book and from his events!